The Peaceful Man

Heal Within Yourself the Personal Effects and Historic Patterns of Male-on-Male Violence

Brad Mewhort

www.peacefulmanbook.com

This book is dedicated to my nephew, Charlie. May he and all of the boys of his generation grow up in peace and live their days in harmony with all of humanity and all of life on this planet.

Contents

The Peaceful Man

Introduction

If you have issues with anger management and are at risk of perpetrating violence in anger, please seek anger management training and professional support. While this book is intended to enable men to heal from violence to much deeper levels than just managing their anger, a book is not a substitute for anger management training when there is any risk of violence being perpetrated.

When I was thirteen and being severely bullied and beaten on a daily basis after school, the violence that was inflicted upon me leaked out through me on to my little brothers at home.

My younger brothers are twins, almost seven years younger than me. As we were growing up, they were sufficiently distant from me in age that we rarely had conflicts. From when they were first born, I enjoyed playing with them, and we had a lot of fun together. I was generally gentle with them and cared about them.

The period when I was being severely bullied at school was an exception.

Just as I was held down on the ground and given

noogies[1] by the bullies at school, I did the same to my little brothers, who were then six years old. I justified this in my victimized, thirteen-year-old mind by believing that noogies would not cause any long-term physical injury to them, even though I also knew that noogies could hurt a lot.

I even told myself that because I was committing much less severe violence against my brothers than what I was capable of doing or than what was being committed against me at school, I was actually being kind to them for inflicting "only" such "mild" violence as noogies upon them. I found a way to tell myself that I was being a good big brother for giving them noogies, even as I savored the power that I felt by inflicting violence upon them.

While I don't believe that the noogies I gave to my brothers caused any lasting physical damage to them, I undoubtedly caused them physical pain, fear, and anguish. Some of the trauma that I was experiencing at school traveled through me to my little brothers. Having been traumatized myself, I inflicted the trauma on to them as well.

Today, I feel remorse for having given noogies to my little brothers. They are both among the people about

---

[1] Merriam-Webster defines noogies as, "the act of rubbing one's knuckles on a person's head so as to produce a mildly painful sensation." This definition seems inaccurate to me, because noogies can be given hard enough and for long enough that the sensation can be extremely painful: noogies can go far beyond "mildly painful."

whom I most love and care, and I feel regret that I was violent with them in this way.

I imagine that much of the bullying that I experienced at school was actually trauma and violence passing through the bullies to me from those who had inflicted violence upon the bullies, in the same way as the violence and trauma passed from the bullies at school through me to my little brothers.

Perhaps those bullying me were experiencing or had previously experienced violence and trauma at the hands of their parents, older siblings, other relatives, babysitters, teachers, or others at school.

Perhaps all of us were caught in a web of violence that came from the distant past. The pattern of violence passed through each of us and left trauma in its wake. As each of us became a victim, each was primed to become the perpetrator of another act of violence to create another victim, continuing a cycle of violence and trauma that stretched back through generations.

The victim of violence and the perpetrator of violence become one and the same. They are different sides of the same coin.

This perspective on the repeating cycle of violence elicits compassion in me for those who bullied me, because they may have themselves experienced much of the violence that they inflicted upon me. It invites me to feel compassion for my brothers, the victims of my own bullying, and for myself, both for the violence I experienced as a victim and the violence I committed.

From this perspective, there's no such thing as simply healing our own trauma and violence. When we do our own healing work, we're also helping to break inter-generational cycles of trauma and violence for the benefit of everyone, so that the violence of men can transform into the peace, compassion, and kindness of men.

While I was in the process of writing this book, Russia invaded Ukraine. The severity of the violence committed against the Ukrainians went far beyond the severity of any violence described in this book or that I have experienced personally.

The relative mildness of my own experiences with violence compared to what happens in war caused me to question what place this book has. After considering this question carefully, I decided that sharing my own stories of violence through this book is more urgent than ever. As a result of the war in Ukraine, I see even more clearly the importance for all men who have had any involvement with violence to heal their trauma from violence and their impulses to commit violence of any severity.

I suspect Vladimir Putin is committing against the Ukrainian people some version of the violence of which he was a victim at some point in his life, though I have been unable to find any documented evidence of this. Without knowing how to heal or deal with his own trauma within himself, he is relieving the tension and uncomfortable sensations of his trauma by inflicting violence against others, just as I did when I gave noogies to my little brothers after I received noogies from the bullies at school. Putin's violent impulses are being expressed against the entire country of Ukraine, with Ukrainian soldiers, Ukrainian civilians, and Russian soldiers all the resulting victims.

The violence of a bully on the playground and the violence of a world leader ordering humans to kill humans in another country have much in common in terms of the impulse to commit violence, the lack of regard for the life and experience of other humans, and the trauma caused to the victims. They differ mainly in terms of severity and scale.

While ending and preventing wars and other severe forms of violence has great urgency, I believe the most effective way to prevent violence in the long term is by each of us as men healing the violence that lives in our bodies and minds at whatever scale that violence exists in us. By healing the violence within ourselves, we assure that we will not re-enact the prior violence with which we have been involved, whether we were the victim or perpetrator. We can heal into living our lives on a foundation of peacefulness, compassion, and care instead of aggression and fear.

To transform our planet into a peaceful, sustainable place for humanity and all of life to thrive for millennia to come, we need for men to heal the traumas that live in their bodies as a result of violence both committed and experienced. Only this can end the cycles of violence that are being passed across generations.

Doing this healing work is our greatest responsibility as men who have violence in our pasts.

Healing the violence within ourselves can be challenging in the culture in which we live. Men who commit violence, especially those who do so in state-sanctioned combat, are often glorified and celebrated in society for their courage and sacrifice. From my perspective, a man's willingness to do the deep work and vulnerable self-reflection in order to heal his emotional wounds from his involvement with violence demonstrates far greater courage and deserves deeper reverence than a man's actions in the face of violence.

We need to establish new standards for what is courageous and celebrated in men. We need to revere introspection, self-awareness, self-soothing, healing, forgiveness, compassion, kindness, and love.

It is up to you as a man to heal within yourself the violence that you have committed and experienced, not only for your own benefit but for the benefit of all men, all of humanity, and all of life on earth.

May those of us alive today be the ones to end the inter-generational patterns of violence among men and to create a new paradigm of what it means to be a man. May peace, balance, care, love, and compassion be the foundation of this new paradigm. May our new heroes be those who have the courage to face themselves and to heal.

This all begins with you doing the work to heal the impacts of violence and create peace within yourself.

This book is intended to support your healing work using the three pillars of healing violence: telling your stories, somatic (body-based) healing, and contemplative practices.

1. Telling Your Stories

Telling your stories enables you to have more

awareness of your history, the context for who you are today, and the choices and forces that shaped you. Telling your stories brings what has been hidden by shame and fear in the depths of your psyche into the clear light of adult rationality, present-moment sensations, and the healing power of awareness.

You can tell your stories by writing them in a journal or by working with a listening professional. As well as creating a narrative of the events that unfolded, it is essential for you to also track how you felt, emotionally and sensorially, as the events unfolded and how you feel in the present moment as you tell the story.

2. Somatic Healing

Through somatic healing, you become more aware of your body and its unfolding sensations. You can become aware of the patterns of tensions in your body that are the aftermath of violence, which enables you to create new patterns. You give opportunity for the sensations that arose and got stuck during violence to be felt, to run to completion, and to release. You learn to regulate your nervous system with greater balance.

3. Contemplative Practices

In contemplative practices, you reflect upon yourself and your past actions, and then invite forgiveness of and compassion for yourself and for those who committed violence against you.

Part I of this book shares my personal stories of my involvement with violence and invites you to reflect upon them to stimulate you to share your own stories, either by journaling or by talking with a listening professional.

Part II recommends and explains some somatic healing practices that enable new patterns of freedom and ease in the body. Historic patterns and tensions in the body associated with violence can reach completion and release.

Part III recommends and guides you through some contemplative practices that are intended to cultivate compassion and forgiveness.

I bow to you for your courage and care to be here reading this book. You are the man the world needs right now. Let's heal together.

Part I: Our Stories of Violence

Most of those who know me today would never guess that I have as much violence in my history as I do. Throughout my adulthood, I've hidden my history of both committing and being a victim of violence in order to be socially acceptable to others. With this book, I am "coming out of the closet" as someone who has both committed and been a victim of violence.

The first part of this book is composed of my own stories about violence. As transparently as I can, I share my recollections of the events and how I felt at the time. I also share as vulnerably as I can how I feel and what I think about the stories today. The names of the people involved in the stories along with key identifying details have been changed to protect the privacy of the others involved in the stories, but in all other respects the stories are told accurately and completely to the best of my recollection.

Sharing my stories about violence is intended to bring male-on-male violence and its impacts on the lives of boys and men out of the shadows into clear light and open discussion.

I invite you to consider what similar experiences with violence you might have in your own history as you read my stories. My stories are intended as a stimulus for you to do your own reflecting and journaling about your own history of violence. Perhaps my stories can bring into your own awareness how you felt when you were a victim of violence or when you committed violence and how you feel about it now.

To spark your process of introspection, questions for you to reflect upon are provided at the end of each story. Please consider these questions as invitations and jumping off points for your own healing journey.

I recommend that you write your stories and your reflections in a journal. While narrating the events as you remember them is important and healing, even more meaningful and healing is describing how you felt, sensorially and emotionally, at the time when the incident happened and how you feel now as you write your story. In addition to your narration of the events, include these personal reflections in your journaling.

As you're reading the stories in this book, be aware of your sensations and stay present in your body. If you find yourself triggered by a story, losing awareness of your body as you're reading, or feeling overwhelmed by sensations or emotions as you read a particular story, please put the book down, take a break, and take care of yourself. Perhaps work with one of the body-based healing practices recommended in Part 2 of this book, or do whatever you know will stabilize you.

Before you come back to the book after something in it triggers you, consider for yourself what it was about the story that was so activating to you. When (and only when) you feel sufficiently resourced and you have had some insight into what was triggering for you about the story, you might try coming back to the story that triggered you and see what comes up the second time you read it. Working through a story in this way can be deeply healing.

If you find yourself extremely upset by a story or repeatedly triggered by the stories in this book or by a story in particular, this may suggest to you that reading the stories in this book is not supportive of your healing at this moment. If this is the case, I strongly recommend that you seek out a listening professional to support your process of healing.

By "listening professionals," I mean social workers, psychologists, psychotherapists, counselors, and certain coaches. If you have not already worked with a listening professional and you are looking for one for the first time, a psychotherapist who has experience working with men and violence would be a good place to start.

Even if you are doing well with reading these stories and journaling about your own experiences, I would still recommend that you work with a listening professional if you have never done so before. It can be deeply healing to share your stories about violence with someone who can hear them, receive them, and accept you exactly as you are, without judging you, analyzing you, diagnosing you, or pathologizing you. This mode of listening is the way of the most effective and skillful listening professionals. The most healing aspect of sharing your stories of violence with another person is to bring the violence out of the shadows and into the light. We can transform our secrets and darkest moments into shared understanding and connection.

When you share your stories with your listening professional, I recommend that you bring an orientation towards exploring how you feel as you share the story, how you feel about what you shared, and how you remember feeling at the time the stories took place, where "feel" in this case means both your emotions and your sensations in your body. A good listening professional will prompt you with such questions as you're sharing, but it can nonetheless be helpful for you to bring this "felt-sense" orientation to your sessions yourself.

This book can be read and explored alongside doing work with a listening professional or as a healing guide and resource on its own, but it is not intended to be a replacement for working with a listening professional.

Violence, Heroes, and Culture

Some of the most revered stories in our culture glorify violence. Many of our heroes, both fictional and real, are heroes because of their bravery in the face of violence and for their capacity to execute violence. The list of celebrated violent heroes is long and grows all the time: Luke Skywalker, Batman, Neo from *The Matrix*, the Black Panther, James Bond, Indiana Jones, John McClane from *Die Hard*, Tyler Durden from *Fight Club*, Wolverine, King Arthur, Aragorn, Odysseus, and Rambo.

In telling the stories of my personal involvement with violence, my intention is not to glorify violence, as is so commonly done in many of the movies we watch, the books we read, the stories we tell, and even the news we hear. My intention is to present a realistic portrayal of how both committing violence and being victimized by violence traumatizes and disrupts the lives and potentials of boys and men.

If anything, I wish to glorify forgiveness, compassion, and somatic awareness in this book.

I grew up in a middle-class family in a middle-class neighborhood in a small town in the mountains of British Columbia. I have a body with white skin and the privileges inherent with that. I didn't grow up in a tough neighborhood of a big city or in a war zone. I've never been in military combat. I've never been a member of a gang or involved with organized crime.

Many people have witnessed, been a victim of, or committed far more severe violence and more frequent violence than I have. My involvement with violence is certainly less extreme than many have encountered, and yet I would still consider violence to have shaped my life in many respects.

Despite having grown up with a great deal of privilege in a seemingly safe neighborhood, I nonetheless experienced all of the violence described in this book. By the time I reached adulthood, I had a great deal of violence and trauma to heal. I have been doing my own healing work for two decades now to heal the impacts of violence within myself as completely as I can.

I readily acknowledge that many boys endure more extreme violence than I did, and I would expect that they also experience even more trauma. I feel compassion for these boys, I wish for healing and peace to reach every one of them, and I hope that this book can be of service to them.

Many men who have been involved in wars and gangs also have undoubtedly experienced much more violence than I have. For these men, I also feel compassion and hope that they can find healing and peace. I hope that this book can serve them also.

The stories that follow are ordered chronologically. They start with relatively minor violence during my childhood and become more severe in my later teen and early adult years.

May the following stories that I share in the spirit of healing, vulnerability, and transparency about my own history of and relationship to violence be a stimulus for your own process of healing.

Sneaky Vengeance

My friend Jerry and I were playing on the playground during our lunch hour at school. We were six years old. Quite unexpectedly, Jerry's ten-year-old brother, Ryan, and four of his friends swooped in and jumped on top of Jerry. Jerry was being beaten up at the bottom of a pile of five older boys, including his own older brother. I was left standing off to the side, unharmed and uninvolved in one sense, but also scared of the violence that I was witnessing, concerned about my friend Jerry, and furious on my friend's behalf about what was happening.

I was dumbfounded and uncertain what to do. Then, I saw an opening: somehow Ryan's head was sticking out of the pile of six bodies while his arms and the rest of his body were pinned in the pile. I realized that if I was fast enough, I could move in without being seen and pull his hair. Without hesitation, I jumped in and grabbed the hair on the top of Ryan's head in my fist and pulled as hard as I could for a few seconds.

Ryan screamed.

I let go and ran away as fast as I could all the way to the other side of the school. My body was trembling. I didn't think I'd been seen by Ryan or any of his friends, but I was nonetheless scared by the possibility that I had been and that Ryan would retaliate.

I felt terrified by my own spontaneous act of violence, but I also felt justified.

I don't know what happened to Jerry after that at the hands of his big brother Ryan and Ryan's friends. I imagine that the beating Jerry was receiving from these five older boys became even more severe as a result of how I had pulled Ryan's hair.

I wonder what violence happened in the family home of Jerry and Ryan. I have trouble imagining that this was an isolated incident that happened one time at school. I wonder what violence Ryan had experienced himself that compelled him, along with four of his friends, to be so brutal towards his younger brother.

As far as I can recall, this was the first time in my life that I committed an act of violence against someone. My body learned through its own action of its capacity to inflict violence upon a person without hesitation.

I was certainly out of touch with my sensations and my body as I yanked Ryan's hair. I suspect I entered into a state of separation from my body when I witnessed the violence beginning against my friend Jerry. I imagine that this dissociation from my sensations was what enabled me to commit so spontaneously this violent act of pulling Ryan's hair.

Questions For You to Consider

- What is your earliest memory of committing violence against someone?

- Have you witnessed a friend being victimized by violence? How did you feel?

- Have you committed violence in retaliation for a friend?

- Have you committed violence while feeling afraid, but you took action anyway?
- Have you committed violence against someone more physically powerful than you when you knew you could do so without getting caught?
- Have you been violent with someone who you love and care about?

As you consider and answer these questions, notice the sensations in your body. How did you feel at the time in the situations that you're remembering? What emotions arise in you now?

Yard Stick Threat

My dad experienced exponentially more violence in his childhood than I did in mine. When he was a young boy, his father was an alcoholic who frequently beat his wife and children. (My dad's father eventually joined Alcoholics Anonymous and quit drinking, becoming minimally violent with his family after that.)

My dad passed little of the violence that he experienced as a child on to me or my siblings. I admire my dad and appreciate him a great deal for how he managed to withhold the vast majority of the violent legacy of his own father. He was a wonderful dad to me in so many ways, and without hesitation I would describe him as having been a loving, caring man with solid principles.

While I appreciate how little violence my dad perpetuated against me given what he lived through as a child, I also want to be realistic and transparent. I did experience some violence from my dad, and this has impacted me. I do think that a small amount of the violence from his upbringing leaked out onto me and my siblings.

Here is one example. My parents considered it important for children to develop good table manners. One particular rule that I found difficult to remember was to keep my elbows off of the table. I just kept forgetting this rule. I found it to be so much easier and more comfortable to eat with my elbow on the table because the table was so high for me. It was awkward for me to scoop food from my plate and get it to my mouth without resting my elbow on the table.

Whenever I forgot and put my elbow on the table, my dad would tell me about how his father would hit my dad's elbow with the handle of a table knife whenever my dad put his elbow on the table. My dad never did this to me. He didn't ever even explicitly threaten to do it to me. Yet, there seemed to be an implicit threat in the telling of this story. I felt tension and nervousness every time he told it, and since I had trouble remembering not to put my elbow on the table, he told it repeatedly.

Even more than tension and nervousness, though, I felt confused. My dad was generally so gentle and caring with me. I truly trusted him and felt safe with him, but his frequent telling of this story seemed to threaten me with violence. If his father had done that to him, might he do it to me? At that age, I didn't know (appropriately) that my dad had been severely physically abused by his father. I felt confused by this oft-repeated story.

Here is another example of my dad's violence leaking out onto me. On a few occasions during my childhood, my dad spanked me for some transgression. When he did so, he only ever used the open palm of his hand. However, there were times when he demonstrated a clear threat of spanking me and my siblings with a yard stick. It was usually on an evening when my mom was struggling to get my younger brothers to go to bed, and she would ask my dad for help. Though my dad responded in other ways to my mom's request for help with this many times, I clearly remember a couple of instances in which his response was to get the yardstick out of the broom closet and to walk up and down the hallway tapping the yardstick loudly on the floor as he gave sharp orders to his children. The orders and demonstration were generally mainly directed at my younger brothers as far as I can recall, but occasionally some of the sharp orders were directed towards me as well.

He never struck any of us with the yardstick, but I clearly received the communication of the threat of being beaten with it.

On one level, I didn't believe that my dad would beat any of us with a yardstick because it would have been so out of character for him. On another level, I did feel intimidated. I felt uncomfortable and unsettled by my generally gentle father tapping the yardstick as he gave sharp commands. I felt scared of him when he acted in this way. I felt afraid for my existence.

Questions For You to Consider

- Did you ever feel threatened with violence from your father or a male adult?

- Did you hear stories from your father or a male adult that were confusing to you because the story and the behavior of the man were incongruent?

- How safe did you feel in your home growing up?

- What violence did your father or male guardian experience himself as he grew up? How did his

violent experiences leak out onto you? Was he more
violent with you or less violent with you compared
to what he experienced growing up?

Notice what you feel in your body as you consider
and answer these questions. How did you feel in these
situations? What do you feel now as you remember
them?

Chose a Spanking

I read about the movie *Star Trek II: The Wrath of Khan* in one of my children's magazines. I was seven years old and fascinated with space, so I was excited about this *Star Trek* movie. I wanted to see it so badly! I had only ever seen a couple of movies in theaters at that point in my life, so going to a movie in the theater was a big deal for me. I kept begging my parents to take me.

My dad agreed to take me to see *Star Trek* in the theater, and we made plans to go on a Saturday evening. I was extremely excited.

In the days leading up to the movie, I twice accidentally hurt my cousin, Cindy, who was five years old and was staying with my family.

In the first incident, I was sweeping the dining room floor after dinner, and I didn't realize that Cindy was close behind me. I accidentally hit her in the head with the broom handle. My parents were upset with me for hurting my younger cousin and not being careful enough around her. I remember feeling angry and thinking that it was unfair that my parents were mad at me because it was accidental and had happened while I was doing a chore that I had been told to do.

A couple of days later, Cindy and I were playing together, and we were running up the stairs. I was several steps ahead of her. I was in a silly mood. I stopped on the stairs, put my hands down on a step, and stretched one of my legs out behind me. I don't know why I did this, except that I was being silly. I suppose that I was seven years old and playing with being a body. Cindy was closer behind me than I had realized, and she didn't notice that my leg was sticking out. Even though my leg wasn't moving at that moment, she ran into my foot, and it seemed like I had kicked her. I was indeed being silly and playing on the stairs in a way that wasn't safe and certainly wasn't smart, but I had had no intention of kicking or hurting Cindy.

My dad didn't believe me that this second time I hurt Cindy was accidental. He said that even if it was accidental, I needed to be more careful around my younger cousin.

I was given a choice between not going to the *Star Trek* movie or being spanked by my dad. I was enraged by how unfair this seemed because both incidents were accidental as far as I was concerned. I had not had any intention of hurting Cindy.

As much as I feared and did not want to be spanked by my dad, I was also absolutely not willing to miss seeing *Star Trek*. I especially wasn't going to miss it for a reason that I saw as completely unfair.

So, I chose to be spanked by my dad in order to be able to see *Star Trek*.

My dad rarely spanked me. I clearly remember being spanked by him three times, and there may have been one or two other times that I remember only vaguely. For my dad to spank me was a big deal.

I remember my dad sounding disappointed that I had opted to be spanked. I imagine that he didn't want to spank me and regretted giving me the choice. He may have expected that I would choose to miss the movie.

I remember walking to my bedroom to be spanked, with my dad following behind me—reluctantly, I think.

I lay down over his lap, and I remember feeling him trembling. I remember being confused as to why he was trembling before spanking me. I wonder now what he was feeling as he had me over his lap to spank me. I clenched my buttocks in preparation for the spank. It was a long moment before the first one was delivered.

I don't remember how many times his hand struck my buttocks, but it was probably a few, and my dad spanked hard. I cried.

Half an hour later, it was time to go to the movie. I was trembling in my body from all the sensations from the spanking, but I did my best to suppress and hide that. My voice felt weak. I felt awkward with my dad. It felt strange to me to be going to a movie with the person who had just spanked me. That seems unsurprising when I consider it now. Of course it felt awkward. However, being seven years old, I didn't consider what it would be like to go to the movie with my dad shortly after he spanked me.

I pretended that everything was normal and made ordinary seven-year-old conversation with my dad as we drove to the movie theater, but it felt forced and unnatural. My usual strong rapport with my dad wasn't there. I think that I faked it well, but I knew that our interactions were forced that evening.

Before the start of the movie, my dad brought me to the concession and bought all kinds of junk food for us. A huge popcorn. Soft drinks. A giant bag of red licorice. A big chocolate bar. This was not typical of him or of my family. Did he feel awkward too and hope that eating junk food together would alleviate the awkwardness? Was he shaken and craving sweets to soothe himself? Was he trying to make something up to me for having spanked me?

I wonder how my dad felt that evening. I wonder what sensations, or lack thereof, he felt in his body. I wonder what he perceived between us.

Today, I remember this spanking from my dad as quite a traumatic incident for me. I'm not sure if it intensifies or mitigates the trauma to know that I chose the spanking myself in order to see a movie. Was the movie worth it? Absolutely not. In fact, I think I was too emotionally shaken from being spanked to be fully present for the movie.

I imagine that my dad wanted to protect Cindy from violence and erred on the side of punishing me (violently) to make sure that I wasn't "getting away" with being violent with her.

My perspective today is that spanking a child for being violent is like trying to extinguish a fire by throwing wood on it. Does it make sense to be violent with a child in order to teach the child not to be violent? I don't accept the assertion that striking a child on their buttocks is somehow different than hitting the child on any other part of the body.

However, my dad, I, and many millions of others, probably hundreds of millions of others (male and female), were raised with spankings administered as punishment for being violent and a wide variety of other perceived infractions. The spankings that I received just include me in the zeitgeist of the violence against children that has been passed down for generations through spankings.

Questions For You to Consider

- What do you remember about being spanked, if you were? Are there any spankings in particular that you remember? What made them memorable?

- How did you feel in your body when you were spanked?

- How do you feel in your body now when you remember being spanked? What tensions or sensations can you perceive on your buttocks or in your hips where you were spanked?

- How did you feel in relation to the person who spanked you after the spanking?

- What do you imagine was going on for your parent or the person who was spanking you?

- Have you ever spanked a child? How did you feel when you did so? How do you feel now about having done so?

- Were you ever spanked for something that you did accidentally?
- Were you ever spanked for a reason that you perceived as unfair? Do you still perceive it as unfair when you consider it now?
- Were you ever punished with violence for being violent (i.e. being spanked for hitting someone)?

As you consider your answers to these questions, what sensations in your body do you feel and what emotions arise? What did you feel at the time of these situations that you're remembering?

Defending My Cousin

One day Cindy came and found me after school. She was upset because a boy who was a year older than her, Liam, had pushed her into a snow bank and rubbed snow onto her face. I think she felt scared and perhaps even violated. As her older cousin, I wasn't going to let that stand. I went and found Liam, who was a year younger than me, and I easily wrestled him to the ground. I threw snow onto his face over and over and over again and told him to leave Cindy alone.

The incident seemed finished until my dad received a phone call that evening from Liam's dad. Liam's dad told my dad that I had held Liam down in the snow and put snow in his face. He also told my dad that Liam's older brother, Neil, who was two years older than me, was ready to beat me up the next day at school for having bullied Liam.

Clearly, Liam had not told his dad anything about what he had done to Cindy before I held him down in the snow.

My dad hung up the phone and came and talked to me about this. I remember him bringing this up with me in a gentle and balanced way. He didn't directly accuse me of anything. He just told me what Liam's dad had told him. Nonetheless, I burst into tears at the unfairness that I perceived and with fear of the threat of Neil beating me up. I explained to my dad through my tears that I only did what I did to Liam because I was defending Cindy. Cindy was across the room, and my dad turned to her to confirm that this was her perception as well, and Cindy confirmed that it was.

My dad called Liam's dad back and told him what Cindy and I said about why I had knocked Liam to the ground and put snow in his face. The two dads agreed that they would each tell their children that there was to be no further fighting or even interaction between our families at school.

I appreciate how my dad handled both the conversation with me and the one with Liam's dad.

Questions For You to Consider

- Were you ever violent with someone in order to defend or protect someone about whom you cared?

- Were you ever violent with someone as retribution for that person being violent with someone about whom you cared?

- Did someone ever commit violence against you to protect someone else from you?

- Did someone ever commit violence against you as retribution for violence that you committed against someone else?

- Did you ever have a parent or an adult support you in a way that you felt was fair and balanced after you were involved with violence?

Notice what sensations and emotions arise for you as you respond to these questions. Recall the sensations and emotions that arose in you at the time of these memories.

A Violent Teacher

I wasn't directly involved in this violence as either the aggressor or the victim, but I witnessed it, and what happened frightened me at the time and still disturbs me today.

Mr. Henry was my teacher when I was ten years old, and in almost all respects, he was an outstanding elementary school teacher. He was creative with his lessons. He engaged his students in thinking critically. He welcomed students to ask wide-ranging questions and held long, in-depth discussions about topics that interested the entire class. He cared about his students, both about our learning and about us as people. He organized us to do projects and raise money for charities. He clearly had a deep concern for those less fortunate. In addition to being my teacher one year, Mr. Henry was also a longtime friend of my dad's. I held Mr. Henry in high regard.

Derek joined Mr. Henry's class halfway through the school year after his family moved into the neighborhood. From Derek's first day, he and Mr. Henry did not get along well.

Derek struggled to stay in his seat and often spoke out of turn. He had limited impulse control when he wanted to explore or was curious about something. He occasionally became excited and seemed to lose track of the context that he was in a classroom as Mr. Henry was trying to teach.

I can understand why Derek was difficult and frustrating to Mr. Henry. However, there were a couple of others in the class who had similar challenges to Derek, and they didn't seem to irritate Mr. Henry to the same extent that Derek did. There was something about Derek that seemed to get under Mr. Henry's skin. Mr. Henry frequently told Derek to get out of the classroom and go home.

One warm, sunny day in the late spring of that school year, our class was outside playing softball for our physical education class. I didn't see or hear what caused it, but Mr. Henry suddenly grabbed Derek by the throat with one hand, lifted him off the ground, and slammed him into the chain-link fence of the backstop. He held Derek against the backstop by his throat for a moment, with Derek's feet dangling six inches off of the ground. Mr. Henry yelled something at Derek that I don't recall and then let him down. Mr. Henry told Derek to go home.

The class returned to the softball game in an awkward silence. I think we were all shocked by what had happened.

If it hadn't been for this single incident, I would have only praise for Mr. Henry as a teacher. However, this assault colored every other experience I had with Mr. Henry. I judge Mr. Henry severely for this one action. I don't fully trust any of my other memories of him.

I wonder what happened inside Mr. Henry at that moment that caused him to become uncharacteristically violent. I wonder what legacy of violence he carried within himself. I wonder what Derek did or said. Whatever it was, I'm certain that it couldn't have justified Mr. Henry's violence. I wonder how this incident affected Derek and how it might even continue to affect him more than thirty-five years later. I imagine that Derek experienced trauma from the incident. I was upset and frightened myself just by witnessing such violence committed by a trusted teacher. I never said anything about this incident to anybody until I was an adult working with a psychotherapist.

Questions For You to Consider

- Did you ever witness a teacher or other adult authority commit violence?

- Were you ever the victim of violence from a teacher or other adult authority?

- When have you felt physically intimidated by an adult?

What sensations arise for you as you answer these questions? What do you feel emotionally? How did you feel at the time in the situations that you're remembering?

Tug-Of-War with Me as the Rope

Shortly before I entered my first year of high school, my family moved across town. In addition to the normal changes that go along with entering high school for the first time, I also had a new social landscape since I knew virtually nobody in my new high school. All of my friends from elementary school went to the high school in the neighborhood where I had previously lived.

The high school that I attended was a fifteen-minute drive away from my family's home, so I had to take a school bus to go there in the morning and to go home in the afternoon.

After school each day, we had to wait for twenty-seven minutes for the school bus to pick us up. I remember the number of minutes so precisely because every one of those twenty-seven minutes was agony for me on some days.

I'm a relatively small man today, but at thirteen, I was tiny for my age. I was 4'-10" and 90 pounds.

My small size, my lack of any friends or even acquaintances at the new school, and those twenty-seven minutes with no supervision by a teacher made me the target for bullying by a group of five boys, most of whom were much larger than me. The largest of them was over 6 feet tall already, and two of the others were not far from that height.

They frequently held me down and took turns giving me noogies.

They held me down, held my legs apart, and one of

them kicked me in the groin with a kick from a running start.

They gave me purple nurples[2] that covered much of my chest in bruises.

They dragged me across the field leaving grass stains all over my clothes.

They took my shoes and everything out of my backpack, ran away with all of my belongings, and scattered them in all directions so that I had to run around in my socks trying to retrieve everything.

They carried me into the restroom and stuck my head into the toilet. (At least the toilet had been flushed.)

They held me down and spit a loogie[3] into my ear.

Versions of these occurred on a daily basis, but one particular day with these bullies stands out to me above all of the others.

I don't remember how the bullying started on this day or how they grabbed me. My memory of the incident starts with two boys holding one of my legs and another two boys holding my other leg. They were effectively having a tug-of-war with each other, using my two legs as the rope. They pulled my legs apart from each other with all of their weight and all of their

---

[2] Wiktionary.com defines "purple nurple" as "the act of taking a person's nipple between the thumb and forefinger and then twisting it around roughly."

[3] Merriam-Webster defines "loogie" as "a mass of saliva and phlegm hawked up from the throat."

strength.

I remember feeling terror. It seemed like my legs were going to be snapped off or my pelvis broken in two at any moment. I seriously believed that I might end up permanently crippled from what they were doing to me. I didn't know if I would ever walk again.

I strained with all of my leg muscles to keep my legs from being pulled apart further. It seemed futile.

Finally, they dropped me to the ground.

I sat on the grass, extremely shaken but physically intact. I tried to act calm, as if what had just happened was not a big deal. Even after an incident this traumatic, I was still concerned about my social image and trying to be "cool." My whole body was trembling, but I worked hard to conceal this. The boys who had used me as a rope for tug-of-war were off to the side, laughing riotously at what they had done.

I must have gotten up and boarded the bus shortly after that, but I don't remember doing so. I only remember the terror of my legs being pulled apart, finally being dropped to the ground, and then sitting on the grass afterwards.

My next memory of that day is being at home in my room. I closed my blind and my door so that my room was completely dark. I hid under the blankets on my bed, and I cried.

Questions For You to Consider

- Have you experienced violence at the hands of someone larger, older, or stronger than you were?

- Have you been attacked by multiple people at the same time?

- Have you experienced repeated violence from someone or from a group?

- Have you experienced violence that you believed might leave you permanently crippled as it was happening?

- Have you ever felt helpless to defend yourself against the violence that you were experiencing?

What arises for you right now as you answer these questions? What was your experience in your body at the times of your memories? What were your emotions at the time?

Fighting Back

When this bullying first started at my new high school, I didn't tell my parents about it. I felt too ashamed to tell them about what was happening to me. As the bullying continued and the severity of it escalated day after day, I finally shared some of what was happening to me with my parents, at least in general terms.

My parents informed the school administrators that I was being bullied, but these administrators did nothing to prevent the bullying that was happening while students were waiting for the school buses. (I was certainly not the only boy being severely bullied.)

Since it became clear that I was not going to be protected by the school staff, my dad told me that the only way for me to end the bullying was to fight back. He told me to choose one of the bullies, ideally the smallest of them, and to punch him and keep punching him when he tried to bully me. He said that once I did that, the situation would turn into a one-on-one fight. He said that it didn't matter if I won or lost the fight because if I was willing to fight back, I would no longer be an easy target to be bullied. He told me that he could teach me how to punch and fight.

Initially after my dad gently made this suggestion, I didn't believe I could fight back like this. Fighting back sounded insane to me. All of these boys were bigger and stronger than me, and fighting one of them with punches seemed even more dangerous than being bullied by them. I believed that fighting back would lead to an even more severe beating from all of them. I wasn't convinced that what my dad said about it turning into a one-on-one fight would happen. I had also never really been in a fight before. I had never punched anyone.

The incident with my legs being used as a rope for a tug-of-war changed my perspective on the relative danger of fighting back. That terror of being permanently crippled was greater than my fear of a fist fight with one of the bullies.

I told my dad about the tug-of-war incident, and he again gently encouraged me to fight back and offered to teach me how to do so. This time, I said yes.

Fighting back still sounded insane to me, but at this point, an insane solution seemed better than no solution at all.

My dad made a punching bag by stuffing cloths and newspapers into a pillowcase and hanging it in a doorway. He taught me to punch to the nose and to keep punching and punching and punching. We strategized together that it would probably be best if I got in the one-on-one fight with one of the two bullies who were only somewhat larger than me rather than one of the three who were massively larger than me.

A couple of days later, I decided that I was as ready to fight as I was going to be. I decided that I was going to fight back when I was bullied that day. I felt terrified all day at school knowing what might come after school that very day, but I also felt resolved and clear about what I was going to do.

As soon as the boy who often initiated the bullying

grabbed me, I turned towards him and threw a punch at his nose. He dodged my punch, retreated a couple of steps away from me, and apologized to me, saying that he was just fooling around and didn't want to fight with me. He looked stunned. He left me alone, that day and forever after.

It only took a couple more minutes before three of the other boys who regularly bullied me circled around me. The smallest of this group of boys was Channing. As the three closed in around me, I moved towards Channing, grabbed his shirt collar with my left hand and started punching him in the face repeatedly with my right hand. As soon as there was a clear fight between me and Channing, the other boys in the group of bullies backed off and let the one-on-one fight happen.

A crowd gathered around us. There were easily more than fifty people gathered to watch the spectacle.

I punched and punched with my right hand, still holding Channing's shirt collar with my left. Channing mainly ducked his head and shielded his face from my punches as much as he could. Through the whole fight, he landed one punch to my jaw, compared to the many dozens of punches that I landed to his face.

I was only 4'-10" and 90 pounds, so none of my punches had enough power to significantly hurt Channing or do long-term damage, but much to my astonishment, I was winning the fight, and unambiguously so.

When the bus arrived, Channing pulled away and ran for the bus, leaving me as the clear winner in the eyes of the crowd gathered around.

I felt elated. I saw myself as courageous and powerful. I felt like I'd found a new version of myself that had been hidden away previously. I felt alive, excited about what I'd discovered.

My life at school changed dramatically from that moment. The difference in the way that other boys related to me could not have changed more starkly from the day before to the day after.

Today, when I look back on this incident, I have a wide spectrum of feelings about it. I still feel some genuine pride that by defending myself I turned around a situation in which I was being severely bullied. I see how much courage it took me, and I appreciate that I found that much courage in myself. I'm grateful to my dad for his insight into the dynamics of the situation and his support of me fighting. I can certainly understand how some might criticize him for encouraging me to fight and teaching me to do so, and I even wish that I could wholeheartedly agree with that perspective. Yet, given the lack of protection of me from the school administration, I also think that he was right that meeting the violence against me with violence was the only way to prevent even more violence against me. I think that my dad was wise as a father in this situation, and I have deep appreciation for him.

On the other hand, I am saddened and even horrified that I was bullied so severely and had to resort to being violent myself to stop the bullying.

I wish that no person, boy or girl, man or woman,

ever would have to fight. I wish that fighting was a theoretical and unnecessary skill.

I wonder what was happening at the time in the lives of the boys who were bullying me. Were they experiencing violence against which they were helpless at the hands of a parent, a sibling, another relative, or a neighbor? What was behind that impulse in them to inflict harm upon someone weaker than they were? What trauma lived in their bodies that they were trying to relieve by inflicting trauma upon my body? What trauma did I myself inflict onto Channing in this fight, even if I was certainly not the one who initiated this violent exchange?

For better and for worse, this fight was a pivotal moment in my adolescence. By defending myself, I gained confidence. I learned that I could take a stand against cruelty and injustice. I learned that I could demand and successfully fight for what I believed was right. I learned to set boundaries and assert them. I learned the necessity of sometimes doing what one does not want to do. I learned to believe in my ability to do or at least attempt things that seemed difficult, if not impossible.

I realized how much I had inside of me, regardless of my physical size. I learned to respect myself and to demand that others respect me. I learned to value myself. I learned that I could feel terrified and do what terrified me anyway when that was what needed to be done. I learned that I could stand on my own.

I also experienced for the first time that violence created safety for myself. This sparked the belief that I had to be capable of violence and willing to use it in order to survive and feel safe in the world. This belief played out repeatedly and strengthened over the coming years. This fight was the beginning of an escalating cycle of violence in my life that would last for the next decade.

Questions For You to Consider

- Have you committed violence in order to defend yourself?
- Have you been in a one-on-one fist fight?
- Have you halted violence being committed against you by fighting back?
- Have you fought back against someone larger or stronger than you?
- How have you been affected by winning a fight?
- How have you been affected by losing a fight?
- Have authorities failed or refused to take action to prevent violence or to protect you?
- Were you ever encouraged or taught to fight by a parent or another authority figure?
- Have you been involved with violence that you considered justified?

- Have you derived a feeling of safety from your capacity for violence?

What sensations do you feel in your body as you consider your responses to these questions? What emotions do you feel? What sensations and emotions do you remember from when these incidents occurred?

Myself the Bully

About a year after this fight, a student named Jackson, who was a year younger than me and much smaller than me, verbally teased me about something. He was a fast and non-stop talker. He had something to say to everybody and about everything. I don't remember what he teased me about. It was probably light-hearted and not particularly cruel, though I doubt that it was flattering of me either.

I wasn't willing to tolerate even light verbal teasing from someone so much smaller and physically vulnerable in comparison to me.

We were just outside a door to the school, and I picked Jackson up off the ground and threw him into a big shrub next to the door.

As he landed on the limbs of the shrub, he bounced up and down, almost like it was a trampoline. He kept talking, saying how much fun it was to bounce on the shrub like that and how awesome it was that I had thrown him there.

I walked away muttering about what a loser he was.

I felt physically powerful to have been able to dominate Jackson, though the strength of that feeling was diminished by his claims to have enjoyed it. Perhaps he had more effective ways of verbally diffusing the aggression of bullies than I did (and I was clearly the bully in this case). Or, perhaps a bully who was more malicious would have been taunted into physically bullying him further.

I wonder what Jackson was actually feeling as he

claimed that it was fun to bounce on the shrub. Maybe he did enjoy it, but I doubt it. I imagine he was minimizing how he was feeling for social reasons. I imagine that he was claiming power for himself through his words since he had little power physically. I wonder if he himself believed his claim to have enjoyed being thrown into a shrub.

The differences between me and those who had severely bullied me the previous year were not wide considering how little it took for me to be goaded into physically bullying Jackson. I did inflict much less severe violence upon Jackson than the bullies had inflicted upon me, but we were the same in our tendency and willingness to find power through violence. Perhaps even the difference in the severity of the violence that we inflicted was the result of our differing capacities for domination and violence. Perhaps I was less of a bully only because I had less capacity to be a bully.

On the other hand, I didn't ever bully Jackson again or commit any violence against him more severe than throwing him into a relatively soft shrub that one time. Nonetheless, my moral high ground over those who bullied me severely was shaky at the most.

Questions For You to Consider

- Have you bullied someone physically weaker than you?

- What was the situation that led you to bully this person?

- What was going on within you that led you to bully this person?

As you consider these questions, notice the sensations in your body. How did you feel at the time in the situations that you're remembering? What emotions arise in you now?

Charged at Me

My closest friend at the time, Shawn, organized a game of road hockey among some neighborhood adolescents on Christmas Eve when I was fourteen. There were eight of us, including Shawn's younger brother, Grant, who was a year younger than Shawn and me.

The game started like many other road hockey games. We were playfully competitive and took the game seriously.

At some point during the game, Grant and I got into a conflict. I don't remember what the conflict was about, but it was almost certainly related to a perceived infraction by one or the other of us according to the rules of our road hockey game. Perhaps my inability to remember the specifics of the cause of the conflict is the result of the intensity of my experience during what unfolded next.

Grant was well known for having a bad temper, so it was unsurprising that he became furious in this conflict. After a heated verbal exchange, despite being a year younger and somewhat smaller than me, Grant charged at me and tried to wrestle me to the ground.

However, I easily wrestled Grant to the ground and held him down for a moment. He screamed at me in rage, but no punches were thrown, and nobody was hurt. I let Grant up after a moment, and he walked away from the game clearly still furious. He went into his house, which was just across the street.

I thought the conflict was over, and we all went back

to our road hockey game.

A moment later, another player called my name and indicated to me to look to my left. Grant was ten feet away from me, charging towards me with a nine-inch chef's knife.

Just as he reached me with the knife directed into my abdomen, I shifted to the side, dodged the knife, tripped him to the ground, and jumped on top of him. I pounded his hand that held the knife into the pavement until he let go of it.

Grant's brother, Shawn, ran over and picked up the knife. Shawn suggested that I leave, which seemed like a great idea to me. Others held Grant down as I got up and departed.

I walked home in shock. Grant seemed to have intended to kill me. This was an act of violence with the deadliest intent that I had ever experienced.

While I was in shock, I also felt a thrill. I felt waves of electricity dancing through my body. I felt powerful. Someone had tried to stab me with a knife, and I had survived and defeated him. I had done exactly what I knew I had to do in order to survive. I was able to tell myself the story that I was tough and was able to defend myself well. I liked that story a lot.

After this incident, it seemed to me that the threat of violence was everywhere. This began the crystallization of my belief that the only way I could be safe from violence was to be fast, strong, and tough. I had to be competent at defending myself to survive.

Questions For You to Consider

- Have you been involved with violence with a weapon? What meaning did you make from this incident?

- Have you been attacked by someone who was enraged at you?

- What stories did you tell yourself or what meaning did you make about violence in the world and how to handle violence?

- How have you strategized to keep yourself safe from violence?

Notice what you feel in your body as you consider these questions. How did you feel in these situations? What do you feel now as you remember them?

The Name of My Crush

I had a secret I believed to be shameful: I had a crush on Jasmine, one of the most beautiful and popular girls in my high school. With her long blonde hair and slender frame, I imagine that most boys in the school had a crush of some sort on Jasmine, but in my fourteen-year-old mind, my crush on her was a dark secret. God forbid her or anyone else should learn of it.

Nonetheless, I took what seemed to me to be a huge risk. I shared with my closest friend, Shawn, that I had a crush on Jasmine. I trusted him to keep my secret.

He lasted two days.

During a break between classes in the hallway at school, right there in front of me, Shawn began to share my secret with our other friends.

"Brad has a crush on Jasmine."

"What? Brad has the hots for Jasmine?"

"Hey, did you know that Brad is in love with Jasmine?"

As my so-called "friends" observed my distress about my crush being openly discussed and shared, they discussed it even more loudly and shared it with even more people.

I felt panicked. I felt shame. I wanted to disappear. As irrational as this seems to me today, I felt terror that Jasmine herself would hear that I had a crush on her. In my fourteen-year-old mind, that seemed like the horror of all horrors.

I felt rage at my so-called "friend" Shawn for betraying me by revealing my "secret crush." I felt rage too at the other "friends" around who were now making jokes about my crush on Jasmine. I felt a series of violent impulses one after another. I wanted to punch Shawn in the face. I wanted to punch Brian. I wanted to punch Martin. I felt overwhelmed and confused. I had completely lost control of the situation. I didn't know what to do, but I desperately wanted to stop the discussion and the jokes about my crush on Jasmine.

Another acquaintance, Simon, walked up to the group. Immediately, Shawn shared with him, "Brad has a crush on Jasmine."

Simon, just orienting himself to the conversation, said, "Brad has a crush on Jasmine?"

At that point, I snapped. I couldn't handle one more person knowing my "shameful secret" of being a fourteen-year-old boy with a crush on a beautiful fourteen-year-old girl. Simon was also one of the only ones present who was distinctly smaller and weaker than I was. I knew intuitively that I could easily physically dominate him. This knowledge probably made it far more likely for me to become violent towards Simon rather than someone who would have been more of a challenge for me to dominate.

I tackled Simon onto the school hallway floor and dropped my right knee into the temple of his head with all of my weight behind it.

Simon was knocked unconscious for a moment. I immediately got off of him, realizing the potential severity of what I had done. When Simon regained consciousness a moment later, he was confused and disoriented. An older boy who I didn't know walked by right then, and seeing Simon disoriented and lying on the floor, he picked Simon up and carried him to the school office. The school secretary immediately called an ambulance, and Simon was taken to the hospital to be treated for a concussion.

I immediately felt extreme remorse. I did genuinely feel bad that I had hurt Simon, but truthfully, I was even more fearful of the punitive consequences that would surely come as a result of my violence against Simon. I knew that my violent response had been disproportionate to the situation. I knew that what I had done to Simon was unfair and cruel to him. I knew that this had not been a situation in which my dad would have condoned my use of violence.

When the school principal later asked Simon about what had happened, Simon protected me from severe punishment by saying that we had been play fighting in the hallway, and I had accidentally hit him in the head with my knee. I was called to the principal's office, and the principal lectured me sternly about how play fighting in the hallway was unacceptable. He said that there would be consequences if I was ever caught doing this again. (This struck me as hypocritical: apparently the principal considered play fighting in the hallway inside the school during school hours to be unacceptable but beating someone just outside the school after the bell had rung to be fine.) The principal's words to me were intimidating, but I also knew that I had escaped much more severe consequences because Simon had covered for me.

In the incident in which Grant attacked me with a knife, my behavior and our interaction enraged Grant to the point that he had a strong violent impulse and attacked me with a weapon. In this incident in which Shawn betrayed my secret and my "friends" were teasing me about my crush, their behavior and our interactions enraged me to the point that I had a strong violent impulse and attacked someone smaller and weaker than me.

A similar violent impulse arose both in Grant and in me.

Of the multiple people I could have expressed violence toward, I committed the violent act against the one who was the smallest, weakest, and most vulnerable. I shared the same impulse to commit violence against someone weaker as the boys who had been bullying me after school waiting for the bus. We shared the same pattern of committing violence against someone less capable of fighting back.

My inner turmoil and shame were more than I could handle when Simon repeated that I had a crush on Jasmine, and I expressed this turmoil and shame through violence against him.

When I recall this incident today, I feel remorse for having attacked Simon in the way that I did because (from my perspective today) my violent response that put him in the hospital was completely unjustified. I also feel some regret that my emotional response after the incident was one of fear of punishment above all else. I did feel concern about Simon's well-being, but in truth, this was secondary for me at the time.

Simon seemed to recover from the concussion relatively quickly, but I wonder how my attack upon him affected him emotionally. Like me, Simon experienced severe bullying in his early teenage years, so while I'm quite certain that my violence against him was nowhere near the most severe trauma he experienced as an adolescent, I wonder if he carried into the future any trauma from my attack.

Questions For You to Consider

- Have you felt an impulse to commit violence when you felt enraged?
- Have you followed through on such an impulse to be violent when you felt enraged?
- Have you become violent with someone as a response to the words that they said to you when there was no threat of violence against you?
- Has turmoil, shame, or other adverse states of mind "leaked" out of you onto another person as violence?
- Have you committed violence that was disproportionate to the actual situation?
- Have you committed violence against someone smaller and weaker than you?

- Have you physically hurt someone badly enough to put them in the hospital? Enough to cause permanent injury?
- After committing violence, have you been more concerned about the potential punitive consequences to you than about the person or their injury?

As you consider your answers to these questions, what sensations in your body do you feel and what emotions arise? What did you feel at the time of these situations that you're remembering?

Baseball Thrown at My Head

Roger was friends with some friends of mine, so we ended up spending quite a bit of time together, but Roger and I did not seem to like each other or get along very well.

Roger came from a family with two older siblings who were superstars as both athletes and students. I think that Roger lived in their shadows and struggled with that. I saw Roger as privileged because his family seemed rich to me, but I had heard rumors of his mother having a debilitating health issue. Today I can imagine that Roger may have had a difficult adolescence, though I didn't ever consider this about him when I was an adolescent myself.

One Saturday afternoon, about a dozen friends and I gathered at a baseball diamond to play pickup baseball. We had all just arrived and were getting warmed up by playing catch.

A baseball suddenly whizzed by my head from behind me. It did not hit me, but it was only inches from doing so. I whirled around and from the malicious grin on his face, it was obvious that Roger had intentionally thrown this ball at me from behind. I don't know if he had been aiming for my head and just missed or if he was so accurate that he was able to throw it to pass just inches away from my head. I suspect he had intended to hit me in the head, but I don't know for sure.

I viewed this as a boundary transgression that I was unwilling to tolerate, even if Roger was significantly larger and more athletic than I was. While I was intimidated by Roger, I was more afraid that if I didn't demonstrate that I was not afraid of him, more such attacks would come from Roger or from others in the future. I had to show that a violent transgression such as throwing a baseball at me would be met with a correspondingly violent response from me.

I was calm and calculating in this situation. I was in an opposite state to when I knocked Simon unconscious. I was not angry. My response was not revenge. I had calculated that I could thwart future violence against me by responding violently now. The risk of a fight now seemed lower than the risk of letting a baseball thrown at me set a standard for how I would be treated. I was violently responding in order to create future safety for myself. I had to show Roger that I would not be a victim of his violence, even if he was six inches taller than me.

I threw my baseball glove to the ground and walked towards Roger. As I got close to him, he raised his arms to defend himself. I kept walking straight up to him, and as I got close enough, I threw a punch with my full strength and full weight behind it into his face. I had recently read in a fictional book that the force of a punch could be maximized by aiming the punch for the back of someone's head going straight through his face rather than punching to the face. I punched Roger with this in mind, and he fell to the ground.

The punch knocked him down, but it did not knock him out. I'm not sure what would have happened next, but our mutual friends who were nearby ran over and pulled me and Roger away from each other to prevent the fight from escalating. If they had not done that, I imagine I would have continued punching Roger.

Truthfully, I felt great after this incident. I felt empowered. I felt brave. I felt capable. I liked that I was strong enough that with one punch I had knocked to the ground someone six inches taller and (supposedly) more athletic than me.

How I responded enabled me to tell myself the story and believe that I could take care of myself, that I was strong enough to be "safe."

When I reflect on this now, I feel sadness more than anything: sad that violence was the only path that I saw at the time to create a sense of safety for myself. I feel sad too that I was a teenager who had a baseball thrown at his head.

Questions For You to Consider

- Have you responded with violence when violence has been committed against you?

- Have you responded with violence in order to set a boundary and/or prevent future violence against you?

- Have you committed violence in order to keep yourself safe or at least to feel safe?

- Have you responded violently in a way that you considered at the time to be justified?

- Have you responded violently in a way that you would still today consider to have been justified?

- Have you committed violence in a calm, clear state of mind, such that acting with violence was a conscious choice for you?

- Have you calculated that fighting at that moment was safer for you than letting violence against you pass without a response?

- Have you felt strong, powerful, competent, and/or courageous after you were violent? How do you feel now about how you felt then? What meaning do you make now of how you felt at the time?

Notice what sensations and emotions arise for you as you respond to these questions. Recall the sensations and emotions that arose in you at the time of these memories.

Powerless

I walked into the boy's bathroom at my high school just as another boy was about to leave. Matt was in the same grade as me, but he was much, much larger and far stronger. He was one of the five boys who had bullied me severely a couple of years earlier. From my perspective, Matt was particularly cruel. Many times, I had witnessed him laughing with delight at the pain someone else was experiencing.

For that brief moment, we were the only two people in the bathroom.

As soon as he saw me, without hesitation, he roughly grabbed one of my nipples through my shirt, pinched it, and twisted it hard. This action was called a "purple nurple" in my school, and it was intended to bruise the area around the nipple, turning the skin purple. A "purple nurple" could be intensely painful when done hard.

With my newly acquired intolerance for being bullied, I was not willing to allow Matt to treat me this way, even if he was so much bigger and stronger than me. I shoved Matt and his arm away from me towards the wall.

My push was about as effective as pushing a house. Matt didn't move. In response, he grabbed the skin on the front of my neck with both of his hands and lifted me off the ground. He did not have his hands around my neck choking me. He was pinching skin with each hand and lifting me off the ground with the pinched skin of my neck. It was intensely painful as well as suffocating.

"Don't you ever fucking touch me, no matter what I do to you," he growled as he forcefully dropped me onto the ground. He walked out of the bathroom.

The front and sides of my neck turned various shades of red and purple and even black. Over the next several days, the changes in color continued to evolve.

For the rest of that day and the following several days, person after person at school asked me what had happened to my neck. I simply told everyone I didn't know. I was too ashamed to admit to what had happened to me.

When I got home from school, my mother asked me what had happened, and I even told her that I didn't know. Even to my own mother I was too ashamed to admit my powerlessness and vulnerability.

I don't know what I was feeling in my body after this happened, probably because I was disassociated from my body and my sensations.

The day after the incident in the bathroom, Matt saw me in the hallway, and just as so many others were doing, he asked me what happened to my neck. He asked in a way that sounded friendly and curious. I looked at him in disbelief. I couldn't believe he was asking me this, and then I realized that he really didn't know that it was his action that had caused my neck to turn colors.

I responded, "You did this to me, you asshole."

He burst out laughing, and he laughed and laughed and laughed like it was the funniest thing he had ever heard. It seemed to me to be a laugh of delight. If my perception of delight was accurate, I would imagine it was delight at his strength, delight about his power, and delight about my defenselessness in relation to him.

He was the only person to whom I ever admitted what had happened.

I was deeply shaken by this incident. The idea that fighting back, whether I won or lost the fight, could prevent future bullying had been so enticing to me. I had fully embraced the idea, but this incident with Matt forced me to realize that there were some boys against whom I was powerless. There were some who would be able to physically dominate me however they wished, and I was simply not strong enough or large enough or powerful enough to offer any meaningful resistance.

I felt shame that I was so vulnerable. So powerless.

Even as I realized that I would never be able to overpower everybody, I vowed to become as strong as I could, to become as skilled at fighting as I could, and to demonstrate with my actions that I was unafraid, and even that I was crazy. I committed to these in order to find safety for myself, in order to create a semblance of security for my very existence.

My capacity and willingness to use violence came to be the only way that I could feel safe.

My shame told me at the time that no girl could ever be attracted to a boy who was so weak and powerless, and as a fifteen-year-old this was becoming an increasingly significant concern for me. Becoming much tougher and more capable of defending myself seemed utterly essential if I was to ever have a hope of having a girlfriend. I cringe as I write this to realize how deeply my shame ran when I was a fifteen-year-old. I cringe at how misguided I was about what I had to do to find a girlfriend at that age. It would be almost a decade before I realized that being capable of violence and willing to use it were not at the top of the list for what most females wanted in a boyfriend.

At this point though, there was still a long road of involvement with violence ahead of me.

Questions For You to Consider

- Have you been a victim of violence at the hands of someone against whom you were powerless?

- Have you tried to defend yourself against someone with whom it was hopeless to do so?

- Have you lied about how you were affected by violence inflicted upon you due to shame? Due to something else?

- Have you felt ashamed of your powerlessness against violence?

- Have you believed that attracting a partner, having friends, or having social status depended upon your capacity to be violent?

- Has your capacity for violence seemed essential in order for you to be safe? In order for you to feel safe? How well did this work for you?

What sensations arise for you as you answer these questions? What do you feel emotionally? How did you feel at the time in the situations that you're remembering?

Training to Fight

Because I believed that my survival depended on my capacity to execute violence, I continually worked to become a stronger, tougher fighter. For a couple of years, this meant exercising a lot, lifting weights, and punching a bag, but I was doing all of this without any guidance or teachings other than watching Jean-Claude Van Damme movies.

When I was sixteen, I made a new friend, Mateo, who had been studying karate for several years. When I heard about this, I was fascinated. I had of course seen martial arts movies, but it had never occurred to me that I could be trained to fight and learn a system to fight well.

I joined the karate club where Mateo trained, and karate quickly became my passion and my obsession. I trained at the karate club three times per week, and I frequently practiced on my own as well. Karate gave me a clear path and specific training towards developing the capacity for violence that I believed would enable me to be safe.

My shame at my vulnerability to bullying made me believe that if I became powerful enough as a fighter, I might become attractive to girls. I studied karate to find safety, to feel safe, and to improve my social standing.

Simon, the acquaintance who I had kneed in the head and given a concussion a couple of years earlier, had joined this same karate club shortly before I did.

I became closer friends with Mateo as we trained in karate together. Simon and I remained merely acquaintances with many mutual friends, never quite liking or trusting each other, even though we were training in karate together three times per week.

Even when I was a relative beginner in karate, I felt more confident in myself and more secure in the world as I became skilled at punching and kicking.

Questions For You to Consider

- Have you done physical training to be strong or trained in a practice of violence such as a martial art in order to increase your capacity for violence or to become better able to defend yourself?

- Have you felt safer in the world as a result of training to become stronger or more capable of violence?

- Have you felt more confident as a result of physical training or training to be more capable of violence?

- Have you made friends or become closer to friends through shared experiences with violence or training for violence?

What arises for you right now as you answer these questions? What was your experience in your body at the times of your memories? What were your emotions at the time?

Provincial Karate Championship

I felt intimidated by the competition in the Provincial Karate Championships. I felt out of place to be even competing in this tournament. I had only been training in karate for a little over a year, and I was going to be competing against people with far more experience in karate than I had, including my friend Mateo.

I only entered this tournament because it was being hosted in the small town where I lived, and it was an open competition: anyone could enter. I had decided to register because it seemed fun just to try competing, though I was now questioning my decision to participate as I looked around at the many intimidating competitors who had traveled from all over the province.

Additionally, in the week before the tournament, I had had a stomach infection. On Wednesday of that week, when I had been unable to eat anything for the previous several days, I doubted that I would be well enough to compete in the tournament by Saturday.

However, by Saturday I felt okay, and the tournament started. Because there was an odd number of competitors, one person received a "bye" for the first round of the tournament and automatically proceeded to the second round. Of all of the competitors, I was lucky to be randomly chosen to receive this "bye."

In the first round, my acquaintance Simon fought and lost his match, eliminating him from reaching the finals of the tournament. Mateo easily won his first match.

In the second round of the tournament, I won my first match, which meant that I would proceed to the third round. Mateo also won his match in the second round.

In the third round, Mateo fought the person in the tournament who seemed the most intimidating to me. Mateo's opponent in this round was more experienced at karate than even Mateo and was fast and huge as well. I was thankful that I wasn't the one fighting him. After a tough match, Mateo ultimately prevailed, meaning that Mateo would proceed to fight in the fourth round, which would determine the gold medal winner.

In the third round of the tournament, which was my second fight, I was against the person who had beaten Simon in the first round.

The winner of a karate match is the first person to score three points against the opponent or whoever has the most points at the end of three minutes of fighting. A half point can be scored for landing a moderately successful punch or kick, and a full point is awarded for a very successful punch or kick to the opponent.

When the time ran out, I just barely won this match, 1.5 to 1.

This meant that I too would proceed to the next round and that I would fight Mateo in the finals for the gold medal. I also realized that even if I lost to Mateo, which I fully expected would happen, and then lost the next round, which would be the semi-final, I would still win a bronze medal in the Provincial Karate

Championships. That seemed exciting to me!

As excited as I was to fight in the final round, I was also scared that I was about to make a fool of myself. It was obvious to me that Mateo was going to win the fight between us, and thus he would win the gold medal. Of course he would win the fight and the gold medal. He was far more experienced in karate, and he was probably faster than me too. I had suspected even before the tournament started that he had a good chance of winning the gold medal.

I hoped that I could at least fight well enough to justify that I had made it to the finals. I was seventeen and still very concerned about people's impressions of me.

Within seconds of the start of the match, Mateo landed a kick to my head which scored him a full point. 1 to 0 for Mateo. I accidentally stepped out of the ring, and Mateo received a half point as a penalty to me. Mateo was ahead 1.5 to 0.

I landed a kick to Mateo's abdomen, for which I was given a full point. Yes! I had at least scored a point and thus thought that I had justified my presence in the finals. Mateo led 1.5 to 1.

Mateo punched to my body and scored a half point. 2 to 1 for Mateo. I punched to Mateo's face and scored a full point. We were tied! I still assumed that Mateo would win, but I felt so relieved that I was doing decently in this match. Mateo scored another half point with a weak punch to my torso. 2.5 to 2 for Mateo, and the time was quickly running out.

I saw Mateo start to release another punch to my

torso. Something strange happened to me in the moment that he threw this punch. Time seemed to slow down, and it looked like his punch was coming at me in slow motion.

Even if the punch was in slow motion, it was a well-timed and well-executed punch, and there was no way that I could have blocked it or avoided it, but I was able to throw a punch at his torso simultaneously.

Just as both of our punches landed, my normal perception of the flow of time restored.

One ring judge granted a full point to Mateo for his punch landing first, but the other ring judge granted a full point to me for my punch landing first. With disagreement between the two ring judges, the decision went to the referee of the match.

The referee perceived that my punch had landed first and granted me a full point, putting me in the lead with 3 to 2.5. As the first to score three points, I was the winner of the match.

I had won the gold medal in the Provincial Karate Championships!

I was in disbelief. Awe. Amazement.

The following Monday, there was an article about me on the front page of the sports section of the local newspaper. My gold medal win was announced during the sports report on multiple local radio stations.

For a brief moment, I was somewhat famous in my small town for winning this gold medal.

The way that people, particularly other males, treated me at school changed suddenly and dramatically. As I walked down the crowded hallway between classes at school, it seemed like a walkway parted for me. I was given space. I was respected in a way that was new to me. Top football and hockey players who had never noticed me before and were giants compared to me would make eye contact with me, and we nodded at each other as we passed in the hallway. I had been admitted into an unnamed, unspoken society of those with physical power, even if most other members of this society towered over me and outweighed me by up to a hundred pounds.

People probably projected onto me that I was the Karate Kid or perhaps even Frank Dux, the character played by Jean-Claude Van Damme in *Bloodsport*.

I loved all of this. I had dreamed of this respect, and I experienced it. I loved the attention. I loved being treated as a respected peer by even the strongest and fastest football and hockey players. I loved my new status. It was like I had a whole new life.

Even more significant to me than the social standing was that I had achieved a feeling of being physically safe for the first time in many years. I had not felt physically safe since before I entered high school. This feeling of safety was comfortable and even blissful to me.

Even Matt, who had picked me up by the skin of my neck a couple of years earlier, kept his distance from me now.

It seemed to me that I had achieved what I had been dreaming about for years but didn't think was actually possible.

As I look back now, I also see that my victory was a

false one. My feeling of safety in the world was shallow because it was based upon my capacity to be violent, and even more so, it was based on being *known by others* to have a powerful capacity to inflict violence. It was a peacefulness based solely upon my ability to be violent and people's perception of my ability to be violent.

What if someone didn't know about my status as Provincial Karate Champion? What if I was ambushed and attacked unexpectedly? What if an attacker was too much bigger and stronger for my karate skills to overcome? What if my gold medal was a fluke, and I wasn't really that good? What if multiple people attacked me? What if an attacker used a weapon?

Since my "safety" was based on violence, I felt that I had to not only *maintain* my capacity for violence but *expand* it in order to be so powerful that I would be truly safe.

I rationalized that if I could do karate well enough and execute violence powerfully enough to win 100% of the time, even if I was attacked unexpectedly, even if multiple people attacked me, even if the attackers had weapons, then I would be truly safe and could be at peace.

My "victory" and this illusion of safety that I experienced only further fueled my drive to train in karate and become more physically powerful in order to continue feeling safe.

I felt proud of myself after winning the Provincial Karate Championships. Truthfully, I still feel proud of myself today for my victory, even as I also see clearly how it was a false victory and had a mixture of positive and negative impacts on me in the long term.

At the time, mixed in with my pride were feelings of doubt and concern that I wasn't as capable of violence as my medal indicated. I sometimes felt like an imposter.

I knew even then that the safety and the status were partially illusions. I had been lucky to get a bye in the first round of the tournament. I had been lucky to fight Mateo immediately after he had fought against an intimidating opponent. I had been lucky to have the referee grant me that last full point when our punches landed simultaneously.

I could just as easily have won no medal at all.

I became even more motivated to improve my capacity to be violent, in order to make sure that all that I had won was not just an illusion, not just a passing moment. In order to feel safe, I wanted to make certain that my capacity for violence was at the core of my being. My identity became closely associated with my capacity and willingness to be violent.

I felt that I had to keep training. I had to keep becoming even more powerful as a fighter. That's the only way I knew to feel safe.

Questions For You to Consider

- Has your involvement with violence or your capacity to commit violence affected your social standing?

- Have you relied on your capacity for violence to feel safe? How safe did you truly feel?
- Have you felt concerned that you weren't as tough or as capable of violence as others thought you were?
- Have you been committed to becoming as capable of executing violence as you could possibly become in order to feel safe?

What sensations do you feel in your body as you consider your responses to these questions? What emotions do you feel? What sensations and emotions do you remember from when these incidents occurred?

Punched in the Back of the Head

On a Friday evening a few weeks after the Provincial Karate Championships, I was sitting in the front seat of a car, out with a few friends and acquaintances, including Simon. Other than the driver of the car, all of us in the car were quite drunk.

Without any warning, without any obvious reason for doing so, Simon punched me in the back of the head from the back seat as I sat in the front seat. Though he threw the punch from seated, it was also a trained karate punch. The effects of the punch may have been accentuated by how much alcohol I had consumed, but nonetheless, I was knocked unconscious for a moment.

I felt angry when I came to, but not enough to physically retaliate or start a fight with Simon. I just drunkenly called him an asshole and continued drinking and partying that evening, albeit with a big bump on the back of my head and a pounding headache.

I imagine that Simon, drunk himself, felt envious that I had won the Provincial Karate Championships after he was eliminated from the tournament in the first round. I imagine that the back of my head was a tempting target to him with his inhibitions reduced by alcohol. Perhaps there was also retribution for when I had knocked him out in the hallway at school a couple of years before.

In any case, my gold medal and my new resulting reputation were not sufficient to keep me safe from an unexpected punch to the back of my head.

When I reflect upon this incident today, I feel sad for Simon and for myself, for the violence that we each perpetrated and the violence we each experienced. I feel sad for the context of boy-to-boy violence in which we grew up, as do millions of other boys around the world.

Questions For You to Consider

- Have you been violently attacked from behind or when you were not in a position to defend yourself?

- Have you been violently attacked by someone inebriated by alcohol or drugs?

- Have you violently attacked someone when you were inebriated by alcohol or drugs? How did the alcohol or drugs affect your impulse to be violent?

- Have you been attacked violently by someone who was envious of you?

- Have you attacked someone who you envied?

- Have you been violently attacked by someone who was getting revenge upon you for something that happened in the past?

- Have you attacked someone as revenge for something that they did?

As you answer these questions, notice the sensations in your body. How did you feel at the time in the situations that you're remembering? What emotions arise in you now?

I Could Beat You Up

I don't remember what was said in the conversation that led to me telling my dad that I could beat him up. I didn't tell him this as a threat, at least not explicitly. I suspect that we were discussing karate. I was probably expounding upon its importance and virtues, and my dad probably expressed some doubt that it was as important as I claimed.

In any case, I told my dad that I could beat him up. I had no reason to threaten my dad with this. He hadn't spanked me or punished me physically in many years. We had a good relationship. We frequently skied, mountain biked, and hunted together. We seemed to generally enjoy each other's company.

However, even as I am clear that I was not explicitly threatening my dad, I have to admit that I relished telling him that I could beat him up. By telling my dad this, I was taking power for myself that my dad had unquestionably possessed as a power over me when I was younger. I was putting a stake in a ground and saying that even if my dad no longer ever did physically dominate me, he also *couldn't*.

I clearly remember my dad's response: "Who cares?"

He went on to talk about how he earned the money and owned the house and allowed me to live there and fed me, and that all of these were far more important than being able to fight. I accepted and agreed with all of this, partially because I did see the validity of his points and partially because I had already claimed the physical power that I wanted, so I had no need to argue anything further. I also wanted to restore connection with my dad because we really did have a good relationship.

It was significant to me that my dad did not doubt or challenge that I could beat him up. He accepted that straight-up. He only downplayed the importance of it.

I felt powerful walking away from this conversation with my dad. I felt grown up, at least in the sense of no longer being a helpless child, though in retrospect I certainly see how I was lacking in maturity by telling my dad that I could beat him up.

I wonder how this impacted my dad emotionally, in that moment and in our relationship beyond that moment. I remember his lips pursing slightly for an instant before he said, "Who cares?" I knew this was a tell that he was feeling more than he was expressing. I imagine that he was quite disturbed when I told him this, especially considering the physical abuse that he had endured himself as a child. I can imagine it being upsetting to him to have heard from me, his eldest son, that I could beat him up.

Questions For You to Consider

- Did you ever tell your father or another adult authority figure that you could win a fight with him? What was your motivation for doing so? How did your father or this person respond? How did this affect your relationship?

- Have you ever been told by your son or another younger man that he could beat you up? How did you respond? How did this affect your relationship?

Notice what you feel in your body as you answer these questions. How did you feel in these situations? What do you feel now as you remember them?

Knife for Safety

It was a cool Saturday evening in the fall when I was sixteen years old. A traveling carnival was visiting our small town, and I was there with a group of relatively new friends, most of whom I did not know well. We went on some rides together. We ate hotdogs. Mostly though, we walked around the carnival talking with each other and occasionally encountering other classmates from our high school. After spending a couple of hours at the carnival, we agreed to leave and go together to a house party that we had heard about.

My friend Pete was going to drive all of us there. He had borrowed his dad's van for the evening.

Among teenagers in my town, there was a game called "shotgun" that we used to claim the front passenger seat of the vehicle. According to the local rules of this game, "shotgun" could only be called once the vehicle was in sight and when we were walking towards the vehicle.

Generally, I did not care enough and did not pay much attention to calling "shotgun." Thus, I rarely sat in the front passenger seat when I was with friends, which really didn't matter to me.

At this moment though, as we walked towards Pete's van, the game crossed my mind, and I called "shotgun" before anyone else did.

Immediately, Morgan, who was walking a few steps ahead of me and who I barely knew at all, whirled around to face me and held a hunting knife with a six-inch blade pointed towards my neck.

"I don't think so," Morgan said.

I immediately conceded the "shotgun" seat to Morgan. I don't imagine there was much chance that anyone else was going to challenge Morgan for the front seat at that point either.

I was only mildly upset and frightened during and immediately after this incident. Though Morgan was facing me, and the knife was pointed towards my neck, there was still two feet of distance between the blade and my throat. I didn't believe that there was much risk that Morgan was about to kill me over sitting in the front seat. Sitting "shotgun" in my friend's van was not nearly important enough for me to take the slightest risk by pushing the issue further.

As I write this now, I wonder why Morgan was carrying the knife in the first place. Why was it so close at hand such that it was pointed towards my neck almost instantaneously after I called shotgun? What was in Morgan's past that made the pulling of a knife, however frivolously it may have been intended, a response to someone else getting to sit in the front seat of a van for a short trip? I had hardly interacted with Morgan prior to this incident and never did again afterwards, so I don't have much context for this situation.

During the following days and weeks after this knife incident, I thought about how I had been threatened with a knife twice, even if the severity of the two situations seemed quite different. I considered knife threats in the context of my belief that being capable of violence and willing to use violence was a necessity in order for me to survive and feel safe.

Since I believed that my capacity for violence was my means to survival and safety, I decided that I needed to be armed with a knife and ready to fight with it in case I was ever again threatened by someone with a knife.

I had a lock knife that I had received from an uncle as a gift a few years earlier. (Lock knives were legal where I lived.) I began routinely, even religiously, carrying this knife in my right front pocket so that it would be easily accessible to my right hand. I made sure that it was the only object in my right front pocket such that nothing would interfere with taking it out of my pocket quickly. I had read many fictional books about gunfighters by Louis L'Amour, and I applied the lessons about how gunfighters kept their guns easily accessible to carrying my knife.

I doubt my uncle would have imagined that I would carry the knife that he gave me for self-defense.

I practiced pulling this knife out of my right front pocket hundreds of times, probably even thousands of times. I could open it to the locked position in one fluid motion with a flick of my wrist, such that I could be pointing the knife or even stabbing the knife in the blink of an eye.

I made clear principles for myself for when I would and would not draw this knife that I was now carrying everywhere with me.

My primary principle was that if one person alone was threatening me, attacking me, or fighting with me and was not armed himself, I would not draw my knife no matter what.

If somebody was threatening me or attacking me with a knife or any other weapon with similar or greater lethality to a knife, I could draw my knife. I could also draw my knife if I was being attacked by multiple people at the same time. If I had multiple attackers, it seemed justified to me that I could use a weapon to defend myself. I recognized that fighting with a knife could have deadly consequence, and these were the principles I created for myself and to which I vowed to myself to adhere.

As I practiced with my knife and considered my principles for when it was acceptable to use it, I truly hoped that I would never have any reason to draw my knife. I was genuinely not seeking to use it. I wasn't looking to be violent or find trouble. I had no intention of being aggressive with it in any way or of using it unless it seemed essential to do so for my safety.

At sixteen years old, I felt safer in the world when I was carrying a knife.

Today, even as I clearly remember my thought processes about carrying a knife and developing my principles for using it, I nonetheless feel disbelief that I derived a feeling of safety by carrying a deadly weapon.

Questions For You to Consider

- Have you been threatened with a weapon?

- Have you been attacked by someone using a weapon?

- Have you threatened someone with a weapon?

- Have you attacked someone with a weapon?

- Have you been in a fight in which both parties were armed with weapons?

- Have you carried a weapon? What was your reason for doing so? How did you feel carrying it?

- Did you have principles for when it was and was not acceptable for you to use a weapon in a fight?

Notice what sensations and emotions arise for you as you respond to these questions. Recall the sensations and emotions that arose in you at the time of these memories.

Chipped Bone

Every winter, a kindly older man built an outdoor skating rink in a field behind his house for the neighborhood children and adolescents to play hockey. When I was sixteen through nineteen, my friends and I spent a great deal of time playing pick-up hockey together on this rink, and I have many fond memories of doing so.

Though we played using hockey sticks and a hard rubber puck, none of us wore any protective hockey equipment. That seems a little crazy to me when I look back on it now, but at the time, it just seemed like a casual hockey game for which protective equipment was not needed.

For the most part, everyone was respectful of the fact that nobody was wearing protective equipment, and the game was played gently, at least by the standards of a hockey game. Above all, this meant that the puck was only shot along the ice and never through the air.

A scar from a rare exception to this typical gentleness of play is still on my body today. My closest friend at the time, Brandon, and I arrived at this outdoor rink together to play hockey, and a few other friends arrived shortly after us.

We were all skating around and shooting pucks into an empty net to get warmed up before we started the game. Suddenly and unexpectedly, my friend Brandon called my name from across the rink and then shot a hockey puck at me. He did not pass the pack to me along the ice; he shot the puck off the ice through the air directly at me.

I wasn't expecting a puck to fly through the air
straight towards me, and I didn't have time to move
out of its trajectory. The puck struck me in my right
shin, and the impact made a dent in my shinbone. I felt
a sharp pain that was overwhelming for a moment, and
I fell to the ice. Holding my shin in my hands, I could
feel under my skin an indentation in the bone where
the puck had hit and multiple shards of the bone that
had been chipped off.

After a moment, I regained some composure, and I
decided that I had to put aside the pain and the injury
to demonstrate to my friend Brandon and the entire
group present that I was invulnerable, unhurt, and too
tough to be bothered by this assault upon me. I ignored
the pain, got up, and started skating around as if
nothing had happened. I played the hockey game,
enduring the throbbing of my chipped shinbone the
entire time.

I never said anything to Brandon about his action of
shooting a hockey puck at me or how it chipped my
bone. Even immediately after the game as we walked
away from the rink together, I simply pretended that it
had never happened.

When I look back on why I didn't ever say anything
about it to Brandon and why I pretended that I wasn't
hurt to play the hockey game, I see several reasons.

I wanted to show the boys there how tough I was
and how difficult it was to hurt me. If I had shown
vulnerability to an attack, I believed that other boys
might have been more likely to see me as a potential

victim for them to attack. This doesn't make a lot of sense to me today as I reflect upon it, but I believed this strongly at the time. I wanted to maintain an illusion for others that I was strong and invulnerable.

Perhaps even more importantly, I wanted to maintain an illusion for myself that I was strong and invulnerable. I so badly wanted to be invulnerable to such attacks that I pretended even to myself that this was the case.

I also felt ashamed that I had been attacked and treated in this way by someone who was supposedly my friend, even my best friend. I wanted to gloss over and hide what had happened so that others, including possibly myself, wouldn't know that even "friends" treated me with so little respect and so little care.

I felt so much shame about myself in general at this point in my life that I didn't expect to be treated any better than this. I expected to be attacked, even by a so-called friend.

I also valued Brandon's friendship. Other than this incident and a few other similar but much less severe incidents, he was a good friend to me. Perhaps I also pretended that the whole incident never happened in order to maintain our friendship—which, today, I don't look back upon as having been much of a friendship at all given this attack.

I wonder what was behind Brandon's impulse to shoot a puck at me in a way that could hurt me. From my perspective, both then and now, this attack came out of nowhere. He was supposedly my best friend, and I am not aware of any reason he had to do harm to me. I do wonder if I had given him some reason to feel a desire to hurt me and attack me, but I can't recall anything along these lines.

Brandon worked a little harder at school than I did, and while we both had straight As in high school, I did consistently have slightly better grades than he did. I wonder if he was jealous that school came more easily to me than it did to him. That's the only reason I can find for Brandon shooting the puck at me that was personal.

I also wonder if Brandon simply felt some kind of anger or resentment towards the world that he lacked a way to express, and for some reason at that moment I seemed like an easy target and shooting a puck at me seemed to him to be a good outlet for his anger.

I wonder what turmoil or struggles Brandon was going through in his life that created the impulse in him to shoot this puck at me.

It's possible that Brandon didn't expect to hit me when he shot the puck at me. It's difficult to shoot a puck accurately within a couple of feet. Maybe he intended or expected to just miss me. However, even though it's difficult to aim a puck accurately, he at least took a high risk that he would hit me when he shot the puck through the air in my direction. The impact could even have been much worse if it had struck just inches higher than my shin. If it had been a few inches higher and struck my kneecap, it could easily have shattered it. If it had been higher than that, my testicles could have been ruptured. Whether Brandon intended to hit me or not, he at least took a high risk of injuring me severely by shooting a puck through the air at me. Whatever impulse he had to shoot the puck at me was clearly stronger than any concern about hurting me.

During the years that we were "friends," this was not the only time that Brandon acted towards me in a way that I can only describe as cruel, but this was by far the most extreme.

When I rub my shin today, the shards of bone that broke off have all dissolved, but I can still clearly feel the chip in my shin bone. Of all of the stories that I tell in this book, this is the story about which I still feel the strongest emotions. I feel mostly at peace within myself even with the stories that involve more severe violence than this one, but this story still feels a raw to me decades later because I considered Brandon to be my best friend. I still feel hurt and shaken that my supposed best friend didn't treat me more respectfully and with more care. I feel some remorse that I didn't care for myself and value myself sufficiently to admit that I was hurt and set a boundary with Brandon that this violation was unacceptable to me.

While writing this story, I realized that I still have more healing work to do to let the sensations and emotions from this incident run their courses to completion and for me to feel at peace with what happened. I have some processing to do in order to fully forgive both Brandon and myself in relation to this incident.

Questions For You to Consider

- Have you had a friend or someone who you trusted commit violence against you in a way that seemed like a betrayal?

- Have you been attacked by someone unexpectedly?

- Have you been attacked in the context of playing a sport in a way that went beyond the normal boundaries of the sport?

- Have you ever been hurt or injured but pretended that you were not in order to seem tough or to maintain social status? To whom were you proving that you were tough or invulnerable?

- Have you been violent with someone who you considered a friend?

- Have you attacked someone in a way that he was not expecting?

- Have you attacked someone within a sport in a way that went beyond the typical rules and boundaries of that sport?

As you consider your responses to these questions, what sensations in your body do you feel and what emotions arise? What did you feel at the time of these situations that you're remembering?

The Royal Military College

After high school, I decided to join an officer training program in the Canadian military. I attended the Royal Military College of Canada to study engineering.

There were a variety of reasons why I chose to study at a military academy, but the one that is most relevant to this book is that I wanted to continue to develop my capacity for violence, based on my belief that my safety and ability to feel safe depended upon my capacity to execute violence. Of course, I didn't see myself as seeking safety at the time. In fact, I saw myself as seeking excitement and even danger. In my nineteen-year-old mind with all of its experiences of being a victim of violence, being visibly and powerfully capable of violence in extreme forms and being able to handle danger seemed like the only ways for me to be and to feel safe. I see in retrospect that this was the rationale of a traumatized and unhealed mind. I was irrationally seeking peace through a path of seeking danger.

My experience at the military college was not what I had expected. Unlike many of my peers there, my parents had not been in the military, and I had not previously been in cadets or the reserves. I was naïve about what it meant to be in the military when I joined. I foolishly thought that "officer training" meant that I would be trained to be James Bond, Rambo, maybe even Batman, or at least Captain Jean Luc Picard. (That sentence is partially tongue-in-cheek, but only partially.)

In reality, the military college was more about leadership and standing on a parade square at attention in a fancy uniform than it was about training in violence.

I joined the military for misguided reasons that were shaped by my experiences with violence as an adolescent.

After completing my engineering degree at the Royal Military College, I chose to leave the armed forces, so I never served overseas nor took part in real combat, as many of my classmates did in Afghanistan and elsewhere during the years after we graduated. I know that many of them witnessed and participated in violence far more severe than that which I have experienced in my life. I wish for healing and for peacefulness in the lives of these friends and peers.

Questions For You to Consider

- Have you joined a state-sanctioned fighting force that has the capacity for violence, such as the military or the police? What was your experience like?

- What led to your decision to join this force?

- How did your previous experiences with violence affect your decision to join this force?

What sensations arise for you as you answer these questions? What do you feel emotionally?

Pulled My Knife

While I was at Royal Military College, I went out to bars and clubs drinking with my military friends as often as we were granted leave to do so. On such nights, I and many others often drank excessively.

On one of these nights, my friends insisted on going to a pub that I disliked and found boring. After tolerating this pub for a couple of hours while hoping we would all move on to a club that I would enjoy more, I became fed up and left. I liked walking, and I was quite drunk, so I decided to walk home, even though it would take me a couple of hours.

After I'd been walking for about a half hour and still had a long way to go, some friends of my friends who I didn't know well saw me walking and pulled up in their SUV beside me. They told me to get in because they thought that it was too far for me to walk. I thanked them but said no.

Three of them jumped out of the SUV, surrounded me, and grabbed me to pull me into the SUV.

In retrospect, I believe that they had no intention of hurting me and were in fact trying to take care of me, albeit in an aggressive way. I imagine that in their minds, trying to get me into their SUV forcefully was an act of caring for the friend of friends.

However, I viewed their attempt to forcefully get me into the SUV as a violation of my boundaries. I perceived what was happening as an existential threat. The three people "attacking" me at once (which was how I perceived it in the moment) likely triggered memories of the severe beatings by multiple boys that I experienced when I was thirteen years old. I also suspect that my drunken state caused me to over-perceive the extent of the threat.

Because I was being attacked by multiple people, I decided that this situation met my criteria for drawing my knife.

I pulled it from my pocket and held it out, prepared to defend myself. I didn't move towards anyone with it. I didn't attack with it. I was completely clear in my mind that I had no desire to use the knife. I merely wanted to immediately and completely end what I was perceiving as an attack upon me by multiple people.

It worked. The three jumped away in surprise and immediately retreated into the SUV, which then quickly sped away.

I felt angry, confused, fearful, and shaken. Was I justified to have pulled out my knife? I had perceived that I was being attacked by multiple people, and so it met the criteria of the principles that I had created for when I could justifiably draw my knife, but now I wondered if the threat was really sufficiently severe. Had it really met my criteria? I was genuinely unsure.

Regardless of whether I considered myself to have been justified to have drawn my knife, I felt angry that they had been so aggressive about getting me into their vehicle. I felt angry that they had put me in a situation in which I felt so threatened that I even considered drawing my knife. I felt angry that the conflict was about something as trivial as them wanting me to get into their vehicle to give me a ride home when I was happy to be walking.

I felt rage, fear, and guilt coursing through my body as I continued to walk, with these emotions probably flowing in me especially freely due to my drunkenness. I imagine that some of my rage and fear represented those emotions re-surfacing from their repression from when I was severely bullied by multiple people when I was thirteen. I believe that this situation had stirred up a great deal of earlier trauma.

After I had walked for another half hour, a friend pulled up beside me in his truck and offered me a ride. The pleasure of the walk had completely dissolved, and I accepted the ride, feeling somewhat sheepish that I was accepting a ride now when declining a ride earlier led to me drawing my knife. I also felt appreciation and relief that he just offered me a ride without any aggression.

In the days after that evening, I continued to feel uncertain and uncomfortable about having drawn my knife. I feared what might have happened if they had not immediately retreated when I drew it. What if one of them had drawn a knife himself in response? Or drawn a gun?

Had I needlessly and recklessly escalated the potential for violence in the situation? Today, I believe that the answer to that question is an unambiguous yes, though at the time I was genuinely uncertain and confused. Today, it seems clear to me that I went into a trauma response when multiple men surrounded me and were being physical with me. The trauma response caused me to over-interpret the extent of the threat.

Questions For You to Consider

- Have you drawn a weapon in self-defense? When you consider this today, how justified do you believe you were to have drawn your weapon?

- Has someone drawn a weapon on you? What led up to this? How did you respond?

- Have you interpreted an act as being aggressive towards you when the intention may have been caring, even if that was not well expressed?

- Have you tried to be caring towards someone in a way that was interpreted as aggression?

What arises for you right now as you answer these questions? What was your experience in your body at the times of your memories? What were your emotions at the time?

Happy Birthday

It was my twenty-second birthday, and I was at a bar drinking in town with friends. With our short haircuts and athletic builds, my friends and I stood out as obviously being students of the military college. We didn't tend to be popular with the locals. Many of them considered the students of the military college to be arrogant and entitled. While certainly not universally true, our reputation was also not completely unjustified. We were rather intimidating as a group though, so it's unlikely that much of anyone would have challenged us when a group of us were together.

On this evening, I decided that I wanted to go home before any of my friends were ready to leave. I felt tired, and I was also quite drunk. I left the bar alone, hoping to catch a taxi. I started walking until I could flag one down.

A couple blocks away from the bar that I had just left, a car pulled up beside me. Three men jumped out. Before I knew what was happening, two of the men wrapped their arms around me from behind and the third one came straight towards me, said, "RMC asshole" (meaning Royal Military College), and punched me in the right eye. The two who had grabbed me from behind then dropped me, and I fell to the ground, the back of my head striking the sidewalk.

I woke up in the back of a police car. It was parked and the officers were not in it. I was locked in the back seat. I immediately started trying to escape since I didn't have any idea why I was there. Of course, I got nowhere with my escape attempt, but one of the police officers noticed that I was conscious again. He opened the back door of the car and told me that I was not under arrest, but he suggested that I stay in the car and wait because they wanted to talk to me about what had happened.

The police car had been parked a block ahead of where I had been grabbed and punched, and one of the police officers in the car saw the whole event unfold in the rearview mirror. The police officers had picked me up off the sidewalk, put me into the back of their car since I was unconscious, and then pulled over the car of the men who had attacked me.

The three attackers were arrested and charged with assault. They later pleaded guilty.

The police told me that the perpetrators had seen me in the bar earlier with all of my RMC friends, and they attacked me simply because I went to RMC.

I was left with a huge black eye, a massive headache, and a bump on the back of my head from where I had hit the sidewalk.

I was also left with a renewed feeling of helplessness and vulnerability, which generated feelings of depression. Even after all of my martial arts trainings, even though I was so physically fit and athletic that I wore a decoration on my military uniform designating my high level of physical fitness, I had still been a victim of violence. I still wasn't safe.

As I look back, it probably wasn't smart of me to be walking alone and drunk as a student of RMC in that particular neighborhood, but that didn't even occur to me at the time. In my mind at the time, I had simply fallen victim to violence again. I experienced myself as a grown-up version of the thirteen-year-old who had had his legs used as a rope for a tug-of-war.

Questions For You to Consider

- Have you been attacked due to your identity, your personal characteristics, or your membership in a group?

- Have you attacked someone because of his membership in a group, his identity, or his personal characteristics?

- Have you experienced violence as an adult that brought you back to violence that you experienced when you were younger?

- Have you felt depressed after you experienced violence or after committing violence?

What sensations do you feel in your body as you consider your responses to these questions? What emotions do you feel? What sensations and emotions do you remember from these moments?

Rage and Alcohol

Lucien had hosted me in his home for dinner while I was in my first year at Royal Military College. He was the uncle of Stephane, a friend and roommate at the college, who came from a small town in Quebec. Since I had grown up near the West Coast and had never been to Quebec, Stephane kindly invited me to visit his family in his small town. My French wasn't the greatest at the time, so I couldn't say that Lucien and I had had a deep connection or even much conversation, but he had generously welcomed me into his home and shared with me an intimate family dinner. Lucien was probably thirty years older than me, in his early-to-mid-fifties.

The military college held a parade and a formal ball at the end of every year to celebrate those graduating. In the year that both Stephane and I were graduating, Lucien traveled to the military college to see his nephew graduate on the parade square and to attend the formal ball.

Despite the formal nature of this graduation ball, complete with scarlet military dress uniforms, I drank excessively. In fact, I drank more alcohol than I had ever drank before. Based on how much I spent and a couple of other calculations, I suspect that I had around thirty-six drinks, though it could have been somewhat more or less than that. Previously, around twenty drinks had been the most I had ever drunk, and being a relatively small man, I was extremely drunk after even twenty drinks.

In my excessively drunken state, I said quite a few things to different people that night that I wish I could take back. There is much that I regret from that night.

However, what I regret the most by far on this night was my interaction with Lucien.

Since Lucien came from a small town in rural Quebec, I presumed, based upon demographics and statistics, that he likely supported the separation of the province of Quebec from the rest of Canada. At the time, this was a hot and divisive political issue in Canada and especially among those who attended the Royal Military College of Canada. Some (myself at the time included) took the perspective that it was treasonous to support the separation of Quebec while serving in the Canadian military.

Lucien was about to walk out of the men's bathroom just as I entered it. There was nobody else in the bathroom at that instant.

Lucien became the victim of my rage about the issue of Quebec separation, and my drunken state left me with little impulse control.

I grabbed Lucien by the collars of his dress shirt and lifted him, not completely off of the ground but enough that he was standing on his toes. Lucien was a little bit taller than me, but he was nowhere near as strong as I was, and he certainly didn't have my training in martial arts. He was also at least thirty years older than I was.

I shook him as I held him up by the collar.

I don't remember what I said to Lucien as I shook him, but it was certainly related to his support for the separation of Quebec, and what I said was probably threatening and insulting.

Perhaps I was recapitulating the time when Matt lifted me up by the skin of my neck in the boy's bathroom at my high school, just as I walked into the bathroom and he was about to walk out of it. The two incidents were eerily similar, even if I grabbed Lucien by his collar rather than the skin of his neck, and I didn't lift him completely off the ground.

A classmate walked into the bathroom a moment later and upon seeing the interaction, suggested to me that I take it easy. This shook me out of my rage, and I let go of Lucien and left the restroom without another word.

I'm grateful that this classmate came into the restroom at that moment and suggested that I take it easy. I wonder what I would have done to Lucien next if my actions had not been interrupted.

I imagine that Lucien was extremely shaken by how I was physically aggressive and threatening towards him. I imagine that he was distressed that a much younger and stronger man had attacked him. He had invited me into his home a few years before, and I reciprocated with physical aggression towards him. I imagine he also felt that his trust and hospitality had been betrayed. I imagine that he was frightened by me. Perhaps he was traumatized by what I had done.

Shortly after, Stephane found me and confronted me about what I had done to his uncle. I apologized, and I did sincerely feel apologetic for what I had done in that moment. However, in retrospect an apology for the way that I had been aggressive with his uncle seems inadequate to me. My memory of what Stephane said to me is foggy because I was so drunk, but I believe he told me that he did not wish to have anything to do with me ever again.

This incident happened twenty-four years ago, more than half of my lifetime ago, and I still feel remorse for how I was aggressive with Lucien. I still feel regret that I was violent without any reasonable provocation towards someone much older than me and physically vulnerable in comparison to me.

I tried to contact Stephane on Facebook about ten years after the incident in order to apologize again and perhaps see if I could make any amends to his uncle, but Stephane seems to have blocked me on Facebook in response. I don't blame him, and I decided after that to respect his desire to have no contact with me.

Rather than seeking forgiveness from Stephane and Lucien, I realized that I needed to work with my own guilt and forgive myself for my actions, even as I feel strongly that my actions towards Lucien were unacceptable and outside of the principles by which I wish to live.

In the subsequent days and weeks after I shook Lucien, I reflected upon how I had acted while I was so drunk. I decided that I could never get so drunk ever again. In the twenty-four years since that night, I truly have never done so. In fact, I haven't had more than two glasses of wine at a time in more than fifteen years, and at this point in my life, I highly doubt that I will ever get drunk again.

Questions For You to Consider

- Have you attacked someone older or more vulnerable than you?

- Have you initiated violence because you were angry about a political or cultural issue?

- Have you been a victim of violence due to your culture or your political beliefs?

- Have you lost relationships with people as a result of violence?

- Have you committed violence for which you still feel guilt or remorse?

As you respond to these questions, notice the sensations in your body. How did you feel at the time in the situations that you're remembering? What emotions arise in you now?

Tooth Through My Lip

At twenty-five years old, I moved to Vancouver to do a master's degree at the University of British Columbia. Just before I moved, I had been promoted to black belt in my karate club in Sacramento, where I had been living. In Vancouver, there wasn't a karate club in exactly the same lineage of karate as the one in which I had achieved a black belt, so I joined the club that seemed to be the closest.

Before I attended this Vancouver karate club for the first time, I pondered whether I should wear my black belt to this new club or an earlier level belt, since the lineage might be a little different. I went back and forth in my mind for a few days. It would be humble of me to wear an earlier belt and give myself the chance to learn any differences in this lineage, I reasoned. I could have a fresh start in this slightly different lineage and perhaps quickly advance again to black belt if appropriate. On the other hand, I had legitimately achieved a black belt in what I believed to be a similar lineage. Why wouldn't I wear the black belt, my ego asked?

My ego won. I wore my black belt to this new club.

In most respects, this lineage of karate was indeed similar to the one in which I had earned a black belt, but on my third visit I learned there was a major difference in the expectations of black belts.

In all of the karate training I had done previously, it was expected that when practicing, black belts had sufficient control to be able to "pull" their punches at the last moment, so that they never actually hit someone during training, even if their punch was not dodged or blocked.

During my third time training with this new club, the sensei was guiding all of black belts in a series of exercises. I was working with another black belt, Ullric, and he was much faster than me. I considered myself quite fast, so I was taken aback by just how fast he was.

As directed by the sensei, Ullric was throwing punches to my abdominal area, and I kept missing the blocks and getting hit because he was so fast. I had done a lot of training to take punches to the abdomen without being injured or even flinching. Although I was unhurt by his strikes, I was surprised that he was not "pulling" his punches at the last moment when I missed the blocks, which is what I had always trained to do when someone missed blocking my punch.

Next, the sensei guided those in the attacker role to punch to face level. Even if he hadn't pulled his punches to the abdomen, Ullric would surely pull his punches to avoid hitting me in the face with a full-power punch if I missed a block, I assumed.

I missed blocking the first punch that Ullric threw to my face, and I was hit in the mouth with a full power punch by a fast black belt.

One of my lower teeth went right through my lower lip. My mouth was instantly filled with blood. A couple of my lower front teeth came loose.

The sensei came by and asked if I was alright. I couldn't immediately answer because my mouth was full of blood. He walked away.

It was an expectation in this lineage of karate that those with black belts could block any punch coming towards them and *never* miss a block under any circumstances. This level of skill and training was beyond the level I had achieved to earn my black belt.

I didn't return to this karate club. I was judgmental about the safety and care implicit in the lineage because they didn't pull punches during training and the sensei had so little concern after I had been struck in the face.

However, when I reflect back on my decision not to continue with this club, I have to admit that another part of the reason that I didn't return was because I felt humiliated for having arrogantly worn a black belt into the club when I turned out to clearly not be at the black belt level in this lineage. I do believe that my judgements about the lack of safety and care had some validity, but they were not the whole story.

It was my ego that decided to wear a black belt, and my ego took an even harder punch than my face did.

Questions For You to Consider

- Has your arrogance or ego led you into a situation in which violence occurred?

- Have you considered yourself strong or skilled or fast and then encountered someone who was much stronger or faster or more skilled than you?

Notice what you feel in your body as you consider these questions. How did you feel in these situations?

Bike Attack in Rio de Janeiro

Rio de Janeiro is a stunningly beautiful city. I was there on vacation when I was thirty-one years old. I noticed a shop that rented out bikes, and thinking that this would be an enjoyable way to see more of the city, I rented one for the afternoon.

On my bike, I rode around in the sun, making my way into some parts of the city that I had not yet seen, though I was also careful to only explore parts of the city deemed to be generally safe for tourists. Nearing the end of the afternoon, I rode into a bike and pedestrian tunnel on my way back to the rental shop. When I was about halfway through the tunnel, I heard a bike coming up behind me at a high speed. The bike was clearly going to reach me shortly, and I felt concerned about there being enough space for a quickly moving bike to pass me in this narrow tunnel. I slowed down on my bike and put one foot onto the ground for stability.

Doing so probably saved my life.

In the next instant, the two teenagers on the bike coming up behind me intentionally crashed their bike into me, and the one on the back of the bike dove at me. They clearly intended to knock me off of my bike headfirst into the concrete side of the tunnel. Though I did crash on my bike and fall to the ground, I was able to do so in a somewhat controlled manner because of the foot that I had placed on the ground an instant before.

One of the teenage boys jumped up, put his two

hands into my two front pant pockets, pulled out the contents of them in a well-practiced motion, and began running away from me. I had nothing of value in my pockets though, and he realized this after running a dozen steps away.

He turned back. I don't understand any Portuguese at all, but somehow I understood that he yelled to the other boy to take my bike. I realized that if they managed to take my bike, I would be on foot in the middle of a long tunnel with two people who had shown a clear intention to be violent with me. I grabbed the back wheel of my bike just as they grabbed the front wheel and handlebars, and for a moment we had a tug-of-war with the bike. I noticed that their bike was lying on the ground just off to the side of where they were pulling, so I shifted the direction of the tug-of-war and then shoved my bike straight into them in the direction that they were pulling. They stumbled backwards onto their own bike and tripped over it. In that moment, I yanked back on my bike and they let go of it. I got on my bike and rode out of the tunnel as fast as I could.

Though I was already exhausted from a long afternoon of bike riding, I kept riding and riding as fast as I could to put distance behind me and that tunnel. Even as I rode, my body shook with adrenaline and fear coursing through it.

If I had not put my foot down on the ground or if had done so only an instant later, I believe that my head would have struck a concrete wall with the momentum of two bikes and three people behind it. I believe that their intent was to kill me or at least maim me in order to steal my wallet and cell phone.

I don't consider myself skilled or smart or anything like that to have put my foot down in time; I consider myself lucky.

I imagine that those boys desperately needed the money they were trying to steal from me, probably in order to afford food and shelter for themselves and perhaps for their parents and siblings. I imagine they lived with a sense of desperation that made violence seem to them to be a logical way to survive in the world. I imagine that they had experienced a great deal of violence themselves, such that violence towards an unknown foreigner seemed insignificant and perhaps even justified to them. I imagine that as a foreigner who did not even speak their language, I barely seemed like a human. I imagine that my life seemed insignificant to them compared to their own daily needs. As upsetting, frightening, and traumatic as this attack was for me, I feel compassion for those boys and what their lives must have been like for them to commit violence to obtain resources.

I feel grateful that I walked away from this situation with my life and body intact. I am aware that a fraction of a second difference in the timing of how this attack unfolded could have led to a disastrous outcome for me.

I returned my bike to the shop and paid for the damage to the bike without argument.

Questions For You to Consider

- Have you been violently attacked for the purpose of stealing from you?

- Have you been violent in order to steal or get money?

- Have you been attacked in a way that you believe was intended to have killed you?

- Have you narrowly escaped what could have been a severe injury or death by luck or by a fine margin?

Notice what sensations and emotions arise for you as you respond to these questions. Recall the sensations and emotions that arose in you at the time of these memories.

Gun Threat in Jerusalem

The Old City of Jerusalem packs millennia of history and barely contained ethnic and religious tensions into one-third of a square-mile. I was in Israel on a business trip, but I had a day off there and was enjoying walking around the Old City, taking in the rich sights, sounds, and smells.

In a particularly bustling and noisy neighborhood, a boy of about ten jumped out from behind the corner of a building and pointed a handgun at my face from just outside of my arm's reach.

I froze. My breath caught. My mind went blank. The whole world seemed to stop in that moment.

The boy pulled the trigger. My body jumped in expectation of an impact, and the real-looking toy gun went "click."

The boy and about twenty of his friends who were watching from around the corner burst out laughing. They were practically falling over themselves in hysterics as I walked away in a daze.

I felt shocked and shaken. My body felt dissociated from emotion and sensation for several hours.

Thankfully, this is the closest that I have ever come to gun violence. Even this incident was disturbing to me.

I can only imagine the trauma and dissociation in the bodies of those who have experienced real gun violence in any form, especially police, veterans of wars, and gang members.

Questions For You to Consider

- Have you had a gun pointed at you?

- Have you pointed a gun at someone?

- Have you had a gun shot at you?

- Have you shot a gun at someone?

As you consider your responses to these questions, what sensations in your body do you feel and what emotions arise? What did you feel at the time of these situations that you're remembering?

Spit On Me

I was walking down a New York City street on a summer day, and I suddenly felt a liquid spray on the left side of my face and on my left forearm. I turned, and there was a giant of a man lounging against the wall. He had clearly just spat on me.

Wondering if it was accidental and he would apologize to me, I said to him, "You just spat on me."

"Yeah," he responded, matter-of-factly.

"You spat on me?" I said again, turning it into a question to express my surprise.

"Yeah. You have a problem with that?"

"You think it's okay to just spit on someone?!"

Getting louder and moving a half step away from the wall against which he had been leaning, "What's the problem? Do you think I have swine flu or something? I spat on you. So what? Do you want to fight?" (This happened long before the COVID-19 pandemic.)

I took a breath and walked away. No, I certainly didn't want to fight a man who was probably ten inches taller than me and outweighed me by eighty pounds or more of muscle.

As I walked away, I felt a mixture of indignation, judgement, fear, humiliation, and humor. The whole scene would have fit in well with many scenes when I was being bullied at thirteen years old, except that I probably wouldn't have responded even verbally back then. Twenty-four years later, the dynamic repeats.

Questions For You to Consider

- Have you confronted someone verbally for being physically aggressive towards you?

- Have you had someone act mildly aggressively or abusively towards you and then threaten you with more severe violence if you took issue with the mild aggression or abuse?

- When have you chosen to walk away from aggression directed towards you?

What sensations arise for you as you answer these questions? What do you feel emotionally? How did you feel at the time in the situations that you're remembering?

Punch Him Right in the Face

A teenage boy and teenage girl sat on the entry steps of a building on another street in New York City. I would guess that they were seventeen or eighteen. He was probably six inches taller and forty pounds heavier than me. Almost all of these extra forty pounds were muscles that bulged out of his tank top.

"Go punch him right in the face," she said to him, looking at me as I was walking past them on the sidewalk. She was slapping him gently on the back, nudging him to get up from sitting on the stairs. "Just go punch him!"

He shook his head, "no," but his gesture lacked conviction. He appeared to me to feel torn. He seemed uncertain and confused. I imagine that a part of him wanted to do what his "girlfriend" was encouraging him to do in order to please her and impress her, but I imagine that he also knew that he could experience severely negative penal consequences if he punched a stranger without provocation.

She grew more animated as I was just past them. "Go, go, just do it! I want to see you beat the shit out of a white boy! Go punch him in the face."

I kept walking. I felt uncomfortable and upset, but I also felt relieved and grateful that this seventeen- or eighteen-year-old boy had the restraint and independence to let me pass in peace rather than comply with what his "girlfriend" encouraged him to do, even if he only barely had such restraint.

Questions For You to Consider

- Have you had someone encourage you or even push you to commit violence? How did you respond to this? Did you feel compelled to comply?

- Have you felt an impulse to commit violence but you restrained yourself? What was the reason or reasons for which you restrained yourself?

What sensations do you feel in your body as you consider your responses to these questions? What emotions do you feel? What sensations and emotions do you remember from these moments?

Broken Bottle

As I came up the top couple of stairs out of the New York subway station nearest to my apartment, my arm lightly bumped the arm of a man just starting to come down the stairs. The bag that he was carrying in that hand fell onto the concrete stairs, and a bottle inside the bag audibly shattered. He bent down and looked in the bag at the broken bottle and then stood up shouting at me angrily and moving towards me. He was yelling about how I'd broken the bottle that he had just bought at the end of his long day of work.

When he was a few steps away from me, I said loudly and firmly, "Don't come any closer to me. I will give you money for the bottle. I am sorry I bumped you. I will make it right."

He stopped and quickly calmed down, shifting to what seemed more like whining about how hard he works and how important this bottle was to him.

Even at that moment, the collision of our arms in the stairway seemed contrived to me. The stairs were not crowded, and I tend to be well coordinated and aware of the space around me. I wondered immediately if this was a scam. However, I also wasn't sure, and I was willing to give him the benefit of the doubt by giving him more than enough money to replace the bottle, especially to prevent him from being aggressive with me.

I gave him the money, we shook hands, and we both went on our way.

A few days later, I noticed this same man walking

towards me along the sidewalk. Interesting to see him again, I thought to myself.

An instant later as he passed by me, his arm again bumped against my arm, and the bag with a bottle in it fell out of his hand and hit the ground, making a shattering sound. He again started shouting at me and moving towards me aggressively.

"STOP!" I said. "You did this to me once before, and I'm *not* giving you money again."

He started yelling at me even more loudly and threatening me with violence, though he stayed in position and didn't move any closer to me.

I took my phone out of my pocket and told him that I was about to call the police if he didn't back off.

"If you ever call the police on me, I will have you killed. Do you hear me?" With that said, he turned and walked away.

About a week later, I again saw this same man walking towards me on the sidewalk. I moved to the far side of the sidewalk in order to avoid the same confrontation from happening again. I had nothing to worry about though. He saw me and said with a big smile, "I already got you, man!"

Questions For You to Consider

- Have you threatened to call the police when someone was threatening you?

- Has someone threatened to call the police on you?

- Has someone verbally threatened to have you killed?

- Have you ever threatened to kill someone?

- Has someone been aggressive with you or threatened you to get money from you?

- Have you ever been aggressive or threatened someone in order to get money from them?

What arises for you right now as you answer these questions? What was your experience in your body at the times of your memories? What were your emotions at the time?

Healing Is a Lifelong Process

I was facilitating an emotionally charged conversation in a men's circle at a community center in Boulder, Colorado, where I was then living. I was forty-one years old. A man in the group cried as he shared about his marriage falling apart. The allotted time for the group process was ending, but I wanted to give space for this person to finish sharing and to wrap up the circle gently, so I had not quite closed the conversation by the planned end time.

At the exact moment we had originally intended to end, two people burst into the room talking to each other in loud voices. I asked them to keep their voices down for a moment. One of the two, Orion, responded loudly that my time in the room was up, and he had every right to be there and to be talking as he wished.

"Just give us another moment, please," I responded.

I felt angry with Orion, not for the initial interruption at all, but for his response to my request to give us another moment of quiet. Since Orion was deeply involved with this community, I believed that he should have understood the potential delicacy of these group processes and respected my request.

I closed this men's circle as smoothly and gently as I could considering how angry I was with Orion.

What I did next wasn't wise. It was confrontational. It wasn't compassionate of Orion. It was fueled by my anger. It was even somewhat reckless. I certainly wouldn't make that same choice again.

I got up and walked straight towards Orion, who at

this point was sitting in a chair on the other side of this large room. "Orion, I'm angry with you!" I declared.

My intention was to tell Orion that I believed his interruption was inconsiderate to the group I had been facilitating. I had no intention of being physically aggressive towards him. I intended to stop a few paces away from him to talk.

Orion launched out of his chair halfway across the room and barreled straight towards me, screaming at me loudly. He was a few inches taller than me and outweighed me by at least forty pounds, and he was coming towards me with a lot of momentum.

In retrospect, I suspect that Orion's intention was only to come face-to-face with me, with his face just inches away from mine, and continue to scream at me. I now suspect that he had no intention of physically harming me or even touching me, though I also don't know for sure that a physical attack wasn't his intention.

However, after all of the violence I had experienced in my life, when he was barreling towards me, I assumed in the moment that he intended to use his full momentum to knock me over and do physical harm to me.

As Orion neared me, still screaming at me, I put my arms out in front me and put my hands on his shoulders to absorb his momentum and hold him away from me. I likely made the first physical contact in this incident due to my possible misinterpretation that he was physically attacking me.

After I put my hands on his shoulders to hold him at

bay, he struck me in the chest with both of his hands, and he began to push me backwards with his full weight and momentum.

He screamed and screamed at me about beating the shit out of me with his face only inches away from mine. My face became coated with saliva that escaped his mouth as he screamed.

My red-hot anger about the interruption to my group evaporated into a cold, white clarity focused on surviving this situation. Time seemed to slow down.

I had a strong impulse to punch Orion, and to punch him repeatedly, but I chose not to follow this impulse. I was clear that I did not want to escalate this violence.

I planted my left foot behind me, which prevented him from pushing me backwards any further. Our arms were still locked as we pushed against each other, but we were physically still now. His screaming trailed off.

"I am going to drop my arms and walk away. Don't touch me." I said.

"You do that," Orion responded.

I dropped my arms, walked away from Orion, picked up my bag, and walked out of the community center to avoid any further conflict that day.

I was more than shaken by this incident. I was devastated.

I had done a lot of healing work over the previous fifteen years to process all of the violence I had experienced earlier in my life. I considered myself to have almost entirely resolved my wounds from past violence. Being over forty, I also considered myself to be too old to be likely to encounter violence again.

Violence seemed to me to be for boys and young men. I
didn't expect that I would personally experience
violence again or even be threatened with it.

All of these beliefs were turned upside down by this
incident. It brought to the surface all of my past
traumas from violence. In the days after, I felt like all of
my encounters with violence from my entire life had
just occurred over the previous couple of days.

Old fears and anxieties resurfaced and nearly
overwhelmed me. I felt in constant danger. Though I
knew it was irrational, I nonetheless felt as though I
might be physically attacked at any moment, even in
my own home. My body couldn't relax. I ruminated on
this recent incident and past incidents of violence. My
mind spun tales to try to make sense of what had
happened and who I was as a person who was
seemingly so vulnerable to violence.

I barely slept for two weeks, and when I did sleep, I
had nightmares.

I felt permeated by Orion's anger, infected by his
threats and screaming in my face from inches away. I
had trouble releasing the black cloud of his anger that
hung inside my consciousness.

I wondered obsessively what would have happened
if the incident had escalated rather than de-escalated.
Would I have been severely beaten, or would I have
won the fight?

Orion was fifteen years younger than me, in addition
to the few inches taller and forty pounds heavier. I
know that he had fairly recently started training in a
martial art at the time of the incident. He didn't have

remotely the depth of experience with martial arts that I had, but I hadn't trained in martial arts in about fifteen years. I believe that I was significantly more athletic than Orion in general, but I was also much older than him. I was still athletic for someone in his forties, but I had less speed and strength than I had had when I was Orion's age. If I had been in my early-to-mid-twenties, I had no doubt that I could have and probably would have pummeled Orion despite his larger size. Being in my forties, what would have happened? This question left me feeling vulnerable, uncomfortable, and confused.

During the period after this incident, I rigidly held the perspective that Orion had attacked me. It was that simple to me at the time. I now see that my rigidity with this perspective was an expression of the trauma from past violence through which I was perceiving and processing the incident with Orion, but I only gained insight into this much later.

I see now that what unfolded was more complicated than simply "Orion attacked me," but any differing perspectives were intolerable to me at the time.

I expected the staff at the community center where the incident occurred to act quickly and decisively to protect the community and me from Orion. I saw Orion as dangerous and a threat to everybody in the community and especially to me. I expected them to set a strong boundary against violence by immediately barring Orion from the community center.

In retrospect, I see that I projected my unmet expectations of the administration of my high school that didn't protect me from being severely bullied onto the staff of this community center. I wanted the staff of the community center to handle this incident with more care and firmer boundaries than the high school administrators had handled bullying. I wanted to feel reassured and protected by their response.

I made clear to the staff that I was unwilling to be anywhere near Orion and that I did not want to have anything to do with him ever again. I let them know that this was not negotiable to me. To my amazement, the staff nonetheless pressured me to have a conversation with Orion about what had happened between us. I became more triggered when I was pressured in this way. I felt unsupported. I felt less safe. I felt more upset. More betrayed. More exposed. More vulnerable. More threatened. More lost. Less sure of myself. Less sure of even who I was.

It seemed to me at the time that neither the community center staff nor my high school administrators had care for me or concern for my safety. It seemed to me that neither were willing or able to unequivocally condemn violence.

While I am aware now that this was mostly projection, it's what I perceived and had to process at the time.

I believe that the staff of the community center did ultimately make the necessary decisions in order to assure the safety of the community, but they did not do so quickly or decisively enough to satisfy me.

To settle and heal all of my re-activated trauma in addition to my new trauma, I had to revisit all of the violence from my past and all of the fears, anxieties, anger, and aggression that lived in my body as the result of violence.

Thankfully, a gentle and caring woman named Charlotte was at the community center when this incident happened. She saw what happened with Orion with her own eyes, and she reached out to me afterwards to offer support. Her support and work with me in the days after the incident started me on a path towards deeper healing than I had previously realized was possible.

This incident with Orion showed me how much past trauma was still alive in my body, and it gave me the opportunity to heal these old traumas more completely.

Today, I would consider myself to have healed my past violence deeply, but I also believe that healing from violence is an ongoing process that has endlessly deeper layers. I believe that healing is the perpetual work of a lifetime for anyone who has experienced traumas of any significance.

Before this incident with Orion, I had not gone deeply enough into my own healing and had not learned enough about healing to have been able to write a book such as this one. The writing of this book, six years after the incident with Orion, is both an expression of all of the healing work that I've done since then and itself part of my healing process. It is the outcome of my own transformational process from trauma to healing and a catalyst for the healing processes of you and other men.

Questions For You to Consider

- Have you experienced violence when you were at an age that you considered "too old" for violence?

- Has the trauma of past violence re-surfaced for you as the result of a new incident of violence?

- Have you experienced sleeplessness or nightmares after violence?

- Have you felt fearful of being attacked again no matter where you were after experiencing violence?

- Have you interpreted someone's actions as a violent attack upon you as the incident was happening, but now you aren't certain about the person's intention?

- Have you experienced violence from someone much younger than you when you were well into adulthood?

- Have you been verbally aggressive with someone that led the person to be physically aggressive with you?

- Have you hoped for or expected an organization or institution to take a strong stand against violence or to protect people from violence? How did the organization or institution perform, compared to what you expected?

- Have you de-escalated a situation that could easily have escalated towards more violence?

- Has it seemed to you that your beliefs and identity were turned upside down by violence?

As you consider these questions, notice the sensations in your body. How did you feel at the time in the situations that you're remembering? What emotions arise in you now?

Part 2: Somatic Healing Practices

Violence happens in our bodies. Our bodies are what violence is committed upon, and we commit violence upon other bodies using our bodies.

It is therefore in the body that the deepest layers of healing unfold.

Our emotional states and thoughts are reflected in the patterns and habits in our bodies through the ways that we move, the ways that we rest, the ways that we are still, the postures that we hold, our muscles that are tense, and our muscles that are relaxed. In some sense, our entire histories are held in the patterns and habits of our bodies. Our every experience from the past is present in how our bodies function and move and live in every moment. When we're stuck emotionally or cognitively, there is often a corresponding tightness in the habits and patterns of the body.

It is common to experience shifts, sometimes subtle and sometimes profound, in the ways that we hold our bodies, move them, and function physically as we heal from violence in emotional and cognitive ways. Healing can also be realized by working directly on the patterns and habits of the body. There can be great synergy in doing healing work on the level of the body and on the level of the mind simultaneously.

When we experience or commit violence, we generally dissociate or cut off from some of our sensations in order to avoid the intensity of the pain, the intensity of the fear, or the horror of what is happening to us or what we are doing to another body. When the processing of sensations in the nervous system stalls, the sensations can become stuck in the body as patterns of tension and numbness, and our emotions can become stuck as well.

I consider the deepest form of healing to be the full return of our awareness to our bodies and our sensations, both our present-moment sensations and the ones from which we dissociated during violence.

Healing means coming back into our bodies to fully feel our sensations, even when the sensations are intense or uncomfortable. Healing is an alive awareness permeating our cells from our skin to our bones so that we can feel a richness of sensations in our bodies.

Healing means allowing our emotions to be felt until they have been felt to completion. Healing is fully accepting and forgiving what has happened in the past, how that past has affected us, who we were then, and who we are now.

Such healing gives us greater access to our positive emotions and passions.

This second part of the book is intended to support healing by providing body-based practices that I myself and my clients have found to be effective for healing from our experiences with violence. These practices are intended to support you to fully feel your body and your sensations; to release the habits of tension and restricted movement that are the result of trauma from violence; and to establish a baseline of peacefulness, stability, and security in your body and your life.

While I encourage you to experiment with all of the practices in this book, it is not expected that every one of the practices in Parts 2 and 3 will be effective for you. While I would strongly recommend that you do one practice daily, it's not necessary to do every practice every day.

Choose a practice or a couple of practices that appeal to you and that you believe will be effective for your healing process, and stay with that practice or those practices for at least a few weeks, if not a few months. Sometimes a practice that is effective at one point in your healing journey may become less potent for you over time. A practice that has little resonance for you now may turn out to be a powerful practice for you when you return to it later on your healing journey. Trust your body and do the practices that feel right to you.

If you wish to explore body-based awareness and somatic healing practices more deeply, you could consider working with a teacher or practitioner of a somatic form that draws you.

Somatic Practice 1: Look Around and Notice Safety

This is a simple practice, but it can be calming if you're in a triggered, anxious state despite being in a place that you rationally know to be safe for you. This practice helps you to spread your intellectual awareness of safety to a feeling of safety in your body. It supports healing only at a relatively superficial level, but if you don't feel at least this level of safety in your body, the subsequent somatic practices in this book are unlikely to be effective for you.

When you're in a fearful, anxious state, your gaze often narrows. This practice invites you to discover a wider, softer field of vision, which can begin to release your patterns of anxiety.

Look from the floor at your feet up to the ceiling or sky, in front of you, to your left side, to your right side, and behind you. Notice your surroundings in every direction, and register that there are no immediate threats to your body anywhere around you.

Right now, your body is safe. Right here, you are safe.

Notice the contact of your feet on the floor or ground. Notice the space above your head. Let the space between your feet and your head be soft and relaxed, knowing that you are in a safe place.

Somatic Practice 2: Making Faces

This practice might sound silly, but some find it surprisingly intense, and many find it liberating and healing. We all have habitual facial expressions that we make that correspond to our emotions and states of mind. The facial expressions that we make can affect our emotional experiences and states of mind as much as our emotions and states affect our facial expressions.

The practice is simply to make a flowing series of unusual "funny" faces.

Look in the mirror and intentionally make facial expressions that are outside of your normal habits and patterns. Observe how this affects your emotions, thoughts, and states of mind. Make faces that are unusual and thus don't have direct associations with your conventionally felt emotions such as happiness, sadness, or anger.

Involve your jaw. Involve your lips. Involve your tongue. Involve your cheeks. Involve your nose. Involve your eyes. Involve your eyelids. Involve your eyebrows.

How many non-habitual positions and movements can you find for each of these parts? How can you combine different positions and movements of different parts?

Make faces that are symmetrical side-to-side and faces that are as asymmetrical as possible.

Make some facial movements quickly, and make others slowly.

Do you get into cycles or repetitions of the "funny"

faces that you make? If so, can you do something different and change the pattern?

You can do this practice silently, and you can also include vocalization. If you do vocalize, I would recommend only making "meaningless" sounds and avoiding words and language.

Notice how you feel as you make faces. What emotions come up for you? How does the rest of your body feel? Some people feel liberated and ecstatic during or after this practice. Some feel anger or grief. Some have memories triggered. Whatever it is that arises for you in this practice, even if it's not much, notice and welcome it.

Regardless of what you feel during it, the practice supports and primes the release of muscle and movement patterns in the face. Releasing habits of tension and movement can be a step of releasing and healing the impacts of violence.

You can try doing this practice without a mirror and thus without the feedback of seeing what you're doing. Both with and without a mirror can be interesting and effective.

If you have a partner, friend, or anyone who you trust enough, you could ask this person to witness you making the funny faces. It can be a rich healing experience to be witnessed in this way by someone you trust.

You and a partner could also do this practice simultaneously, such that you're making funny faces at each other and riffing off the faces that you're witnessing in the other person.

I consider making funny faces to be a potent healing practice, but if it seems silly to you or you feel uncomfortable doing it, you might want to jump to practice 4 for a more meditative practice.

Somatic Practice 3: Follow the Impulses of Your Body into Movement

This practice brings the principles of the "Funny Faces" practice to your entire body. We all have habitual patterns of muscular engagement, tensions, and movements in our bodies. In this practice, we seek to be sensitive to the sensations of the body and to "listen" to these sensations to invite non-habitual movements and muscular engagement. In doing so, we release tension and restrictions that were formed during our encounters with violence.

Clear a space on the floor in which you'll be able to move around. It should ideally be large enough for you to jump and roll around, and it must be clear of anything sharp or dangerous.

You can start this practice in any position you choose. I like to start it standing with my eyes closed. I notice the feeling of the contact of my feet on the floor. I notice the subtle shifts that happen in my ankles, knees, and hips to maintain my balance. I notice the movement of my ribs and diaphragm with my breath. I notice my head balanced on top of my neck.

Then, I tune in to any impulse for movement that arises in my body. How does my body want to move? It could be an impulse for a simple movement, such as a small swinging of one arm or a rotation of my head. It could be a larger movement like a jump in the air or getting down on the floor and rolling. It could be an impulse to move one part of the body or the whole body.

Whatever impulse for movement you feel, open your eyes (for your safety) and follow that impulse (within the bounds of safety).

As you follow your movement impulse, what do you feel? What bodily impulse arises in response to that movement? Notice what sensations and emotions emerge in response to following the movement impulse. Feeling those sensations or emotions, what is your next movement impulse? Keep following whatever impulse for movement arises in you.

To shake the body is a common impulse that has the potential for loosening stuck tensions and habits.

You can include making sounds with your movements. You can even speak in tongues, which means making speech-like sounds that don't have any meaning to you.

You can include moving your face such as you did in the previous practice along with the other movements of your body.

Staying still is another valid impulse to follow.

Sometimes your series of movements might look like a dance. Sometimes they might look like a tantrum that a two-year old might have. It can look like anything, and it doesn't matter what it looks like. Keep your awareness focused on the sensations in your body and your impulses for movement; don't worry about how you or your movements look.

I've been asked many times if this practice can be done with music on. While it can be, I don't recommend it. When this practice is done with music, the movements tend to become strongly influenced by the music, even if you're not consciously dancing to it. Ideally, the movements that you make in this practice are informed by your sensations and the movement impulses that arise from your sensations. That's difficult to do when music is playing.

Keep following movement impulse after movement impulse until you have the impulse to be complete or until you reach the end of a time that you have allotted for this practice.

Though this practice can seem simple and light, it can invite some intense experiences for some people. It certainly has for me, in both adverse and ecstatic ways. I have spent many hundreds of hours doing this practice over the course of more than a decade.

Do this practice with as much awareness of your whole body and your sensations and emotions as you can maintain, and also be gentle with yourself, physically and emotionally.

Somatic Practice 4: Box Breathing

This breathing practice, often referred to as box breathing, is used by the United States Navy Seals both as a daily practice and right before and during missions to help them to be simultaneously calm and alert. Likely, box breathing has been used in conjunction with a great deal of violence. That's almost reason enough for me to avoid this practice altogether, but I also like the idea of "reclaiming" the practice in service of peace and healing. After all, feeling calm and alert simultaneously is a powerful state for doing healing work, and box breathing is a potent tool for reaching such a state.

This is the box breathing process:

1. Slowly inhale through your nose to fill your lungs as you count to four.

2. Once your lungs are full, hold your breath as you count to four.

3. Slowly exhale out your nose to empty your lungs as you count to four.

4. Once your lungs are empty, hold your breath as you count to four.

5. Go back to #1 and repeat this cycle for several minutes or for as long as you wish.

Close your eyes when you do this practice and focus your attention on the movement of the breath through your nose.

Once you're comfortable doing box breathing on a count of four, increase your count for all four of the steps to five, and then to six, and further if you can.

However, only increase the count once you're relatively comfortable with the current length you're doing. It's okay if you feel a slight hunger for air during the breath holds, but you also should be able to remain soft and relaxed in your body throughout the cycles. Notice if you tense your jaw, your tongue, your abdomen, or your face.

If you gasp for air at any point, the count that you're doing is too long for you for right now.

By working to increase the count that you're doing at each step, you're increasing your carbon dioxide tolerance, which supports emotional resilience and reduces fear and anxiety.

Both the inhales and exhales should be through your nose only. If you breathe through your mouth, you're missing out on many of the benefits of the practice.

We generally breath through our mouths when we're afraid, and doing so tends to exacerbate fear and anxiety. Mouth breathing stimulates the sympathetic nervous system, which is the aspect of the nervous system that puts us into a "fight or flight" state.

During violence, we sometimes start mouth breathing due to fear, and trauma can cause this way of breathing to become stuck and hold us in a state of habitual anxiety. By box breathing through the nose only, we change this habit to calming, healthier nasal breathing.

To read more about the importance of nasal breathing and the benefits of it, I recommend the book *Breath: The New Science of a Lost Art* by James Nestor.

Somatic Practice 5: Spaces Between

An audio narration of this practice is available on the "Resources" page of www.peacefulmanbook.com. It can also be accessed directly by scanning this QR code.

This practice is intended to invite softness, spaciousness, and ease into your body. It breaks habits of tension in your body that may result from your exposure to violence or other traumas.

This practice requires the discipline and focus of a meditation to do it well. It can seem repetitive as you first learn it. However, I consider this to be a potent practice, especially if you practice it consistently over a long period of time. I do this practice daily and have for more than a decade; it helps me to feel grounded, soft, and present in my body, which is exactly how I like to start my mornings.

Start by sitting in a comfortable position. If you have an inclination towards formal meditation positions or sitting on a meditation cushion, those are great for this practice. You can also do this practice in a comfortable armchair or anything in between.

Notice the outside of your right shoulder and the outside of your left shoulder. Notice the space in between your two shoulders. Without making any movement whatsoever, "think" your two shoulders releasing away from each other. Let all of the space in between your two shoulders be soft. "Think" softness into this space.

Notice the right side of your hips and the left side of your hips. Notice the space between them. "Think" softness into all of that space. Without making any movement at all, "think" your hips softening.

Notice your left ear. Notice your right ear. Notice the space between your two ears, right through your head. Let this space between your ears be soft. Think your two ears releasing away from each other to create spaciousness and softness between the two sides of your head.

Bring awareness to the back of your head and the tip of your nose. Be aware of the space in your head between your nose and the back of your head, and let this space soften. Let the front and the back of your head release away from each other to create spaciousness, without making any movement. Just think the release.

Notice your chin and the top of your head and the space between the two. Let this space be soft. Allow the top of your head to release upwards away from your chin just by thinking this, without making any actual movement or using any muscles.

Notice your jaw joints on both the right and left sides. Allow the joint on the left to soften. Allow the joint on the right to soften. You might lightly place a finger upon these joints as you invite them to soften to create sensory feedback for yourself about where these joints are located.

Notice your tongue and let it soften.

Notice your left eye and let it soften.

Notice your right eye and let it soften.

Notice the space between your two eyes.

The physical space inside your head should feel lighter, softer, and more spacious at this point.

Bring your awareness to your hips again. Allow your hips to soften and spread into the contact that they are making with the surface of your seat. Notice the space between the surface that your hips are touching and the top of your head. Notice this whole span from your hips, up through your spine, through your abdomen, through your chest, through your neck, through your head to the top of your head. As you notice the distance between your contact with the seat and the crown of your head, let this whole space between the two soften. By softening and thinking into release rather than engaging any muscles, allow the expanse of the spine to release into length.

Notice the space between the left side of your rib cage and the right side. Let this space through your chest, including your heart and lungs, be soft. Allow these two sides of your torso to release away from each other. You could also think about this as allowing your back to release into width.

Notice the space between your upper back and the front of your chest, again observing that your heart and lungs are inside of this space. Let this space soften, and notice the physical distance between your chest and your back.

Notice the space between your lower back and the front of your abdomen. Let your abdomen be soft. A lot of tension can unconsciously be held in the abdomen, so take an extra moment here and keep asking your abdominal muscles to release and soften. Notice the space that your abdomen occupies, and think lightness and fluidity in that space.

Notice the space between your right hip and your right knee, and release this span into length, not by doing anything but simply by thinking a release. Think softness in your right hip and softness in your right knee. Infuse your right leg between your hip and knee with softness.

Notice the space between your left hip and your left knee, and release this span into length, not by doing anything but simply by thinking a release. Think softness in your left hip and softness in your left knee. Infuse your left leg between your hip and knee with softness.

Notice the space between your right knee and your right heel. Allow your knee and heal to release away from each other, not by doing anything, but by just thinking the softening of your lower leg and releasing your right lower leg into length.

Notice the space between your left knee and your left heel. Allow your knee and heal to release away from each other, not by doing anything, but by just thinking the softening of your lower leg and releasing your left lower leg into length.

Your right foot has length from your heel to your toes and width between the inside and outside of your foot. Let your right foot release into both widening and lengthening. Without physically making any motion or engaging any muscles, think your right foot stretching into length and width as an invitation for it to soften and release.

Your left foot also has length from your heel to your toes and width between the inside and outside of your foot. Let your left foot release into both widening and lengthening. Without physically making any motion or engaging any muscles, think your left foot stretching into length and width as an invitation for it to soften and release.

Hold in awareness your right shoulder and right elbow; notice the space between the two. Invite softness into that span. Without physically doing anything, allow your right shoulder and right elbow to release away from each other, just by allowing it in your mind.

Bring into your awareness your left shoulder and left elbow; notice the space between the two. Invite softness into that span. Without physically doing anything, allow your left shoulder and left elbow to release away from each other, just by allowing it in your mind.

Notice the space from your right elbow to your right small finger, your right elbow to your right ring finger, your right elbow to your right middle finger, your right elbow to your right index finger, and your right elbow to your right thumb. For each of these spans, allow the full distance between your elbow and the tip of each finger to be soft and to release into length.

Notice the spaces on your right hand between your thumb and index finger, index finger and middle finger, middle finger and ring finger, and ring finger and small finger. Invite softness into each of these spaces between your fingers on your right hand.

Notice the space from your left elbow to your left

small finger, your left elbow to your left ring finger, your left elbow to your left middle finger, your left elbow to your left index finger, and your left elbow to your left thumb. For each of these spans, allow the full distance between your elbow and the tip of each finger to be soft and to release into length.

Notice the spaces on your left hand between your thumb and index finger, index finger and middle finger, middle finger and ring finger, and ring finger and small finger. Invite softness into each of these spaces between your fingers on your left hand.

Bring into your awareness the top of your head and both of your shoulders. Be aware of the triangular space formed by your two shoulders and the top of your head. Let this space be soft. In your mind, let the triangle release into expansion to become a larger triangle, without making any physical movement.

Notice your hips and the top of your head, and let the space between them soften.

Be aware of the physical locations of your heels and of your hips. Invite softening into the space between them.

Hold in your awareness the physical locations of the top of your head and of your heels. Allow that whole span through your body to spread by thinking a release into softness, without making any physical movement or engaging any muscles.

How does your body feel now? What is your state of mind now?

Somatic Practice 6: Alternate Nostril Breathing

Alternate nostril breathing, originally a yogic practice, has a much gentler origin than the Navy Seal's box breathing. It can be a basic and gentle breathing practice or an advanced and intense breathing practice depending on the way that it is practiced. Choose a version that feels right for you.

Many find it beneficial to practice Box Breathing and the Spaces Between practice for a while before doing alternative nostril breathing.

Here are the steps for a basic version of this practice:

1. Sit in a way that is comfortable for you. Yogis sit in full lotus. I often sit in an armchair.

2. After an exhale, pinch your nose gently but firmly enough to prevent air from passing. Keep your mouth closed. Count to eight.

3. Open your left nostril and inhale on a count of 4.

4. Pinch both nostrils after the inhale and count to 4.

5. Open your right nostril and exhale on a count of 4.

6. Pinch both nostrils after the exhale and count to 8.

7. Open your right nostril and inhale on a count of 4.

8. Pinch both nostrils after the inhale and count to 4.

9. Open your left nostril and exhale on a count of 4.

10. Pinch both nostrils and count to 8.

11. Return to step 3.

As you do this practice, keep softening and relaxing your body, such as is described in the spaces between practice. Notice especially your tongue, your jaw, and your neck, which often tense during breathing practices. Notice your chest and abdomen. Keep softening these parts along with the rest of your body.

When this basic version of the practice is smooth for you, you know the flow of the breaths without thought, and you don't feel out of breath with the counts described above, you can begin to extend the count of the exhalations to eight and the retentions as much as you are able to do reasonably comfortably. You can experiment and play with the counts in infinite ways to see what effects different counts have.

As a general guideline, keep the counts on the retentions after the exhalations at least as long or longer than the counts for any other segment.

For example, these are the counts that I often do:
1. After an exhalation, hold for a count of 20.
2. Left nostril inhalation on a count of 4.
3. After inhalation, hold for a count of 20.
4. Right nostril exhalation on a count of 8.
5. After exhalation, hold for a count of 20.
6. Right nostril inhalation on a count of 4.
7. After inhalation, hold for a count of 20.
8. Left nostril exhalation on a count of 8.
9. Return to step 1.

For "counts," I count my heartbeats. Doing so brings awareness to the pumping of my heart, increasing my overall somatic awareness. If it isn't easy for you to hear or feel your own heartbeat, just count in a way that seems relatively consistent to you. After doing this and other body-based practices recommended in this book consistently for a while, you may organically begin to hear or feel your heartbeat.

While alternate nostril breathing should leave you feeling peaceful and refreshed after you do it even for the first time, the most benefit from this practice comes from practicing it every day for a long time. I fell in love with this practice after doing it almost daily for more than a year.

Somatic Practice 7: Sensation Exploration

Many people find it challenging to feel the nuances of the sensations in their bodies at first when doing this practice. I did when I first learned it. The difficulty is common in our modern society in general and even more common among those of us who have experienced trauma due to violence. However, feeling your sensations and being able to label and follow them is learnable by virtually everyone, especially if you stay with it and are patient with yourself. Working individually with a somatically-oriented listening professional to guide you through the process can be supportive as well if this practice draws you.

To start this practice, notice any sensation in your body. Keep your attention on that sensation. Hold it in your awareness.

How would you describe the sensation?

What is the shape of the sensation?

What is its texture or consistency of it?

How dense or light is it?

Is there a push or a pull associated with the sensation?

Where are the edges of the sensation, and what do the edges feel like?

Does the sensation move around inside your body?

Does the sensation morph in shape? Does it vibrate? Or flow?

What color is the sensation? How bright or dark is it?

How does the sensation change as you keep it in awareness?

What sound does the sensation make?

Does the sensation have an emotional quality?

What does this sensation need or want? What impulse does it have?

From where does this sensation come?

Where does this sensation belong?

What would this sensation like to have as a name?

What message or information does the sensation have for you?

Again, how does the sensation change as you hold it in awareness?

These questions are intended to enable you to get to know this sensation and the emotions, thoughts, and wants or needs associated with it.

Sometimes a sensation will point to another sensation elsewhere in the body, and sometimes awareness will organically shift to a different sensation. You can follow the sensations as they arise in this exploration, but notice if you're avoiding awareness of a sensation that is unpleasant or uncomfortable.

Part 3: Contemplative Healing Practices

The following contemplative practices are intended to develop compassion, forgiveness, and clarity about your principles in regard to violence. After you become clear about the principles by which you want to live your life, you will be ready to invite forgiveness and compassion.

By first working on your personal principles in relation to violence and then practicing compassion and forgiveness, you can fully feel the emotional impacts of your past involvement with violence, acknowledge what actions (taken by others or yourself) were out of alignment with your principles, and forgive and feel compassion for yourself and for others for involvement with violence, even if that involvement was out of alignment with your principles.

Contemplative Practice 1: Clarity About Your Principles

Your principles are your intentions for how you want to act based upon who you want to be, how you want to live your life, and what you believe to be right and wrong. They are commitments for how you will choose to act, even when doing so may be difficult.

It's possible for situations to arise in which you are clear about your principles, but you don't have the capacity or willpower to act in alignment with them. You can use such situations to strengthen your resolve for acting in alignment with your principles or to refine your principles to better guide and support you, depending on what is appropriate for the situation.

Before you explore forgiveness of yourself and others, it is best for you to have clarity about your principles regarding violence. Become clear about when you consider violence to be unacceptable, and then take an honest inventory of how your past actions and involvement with violence have stacked up against the principles you hold.

If you practice forgiveness and compassion without already having clarity about how your past actions have deviated from your principles, the practices of forgiveness and compassion may imply that the violence you committed was acceptable.

We ideally want to be clear about when and how we acted out of alignment with our principles in the past, to fully feel our sensations and emotions related to this, and then to invite forgiveness and compassion for ourselves and others.

We want to forgive and have compassion for violence that is unacceptable according to our principles without in any way condoning the violence. Both our principles and our forgiveness can then be clear and deep.

As examples of what your principles regarding violence and your more general principles might look like, here are some principles that I hold.

I aspire and hope to never again take any violent action against any human for the rest of my life, and yet there are circumstances in which I would do so and in which doing so would be within my principles.

If someone attacked me violently, I would fight back. If someone violently attacked my wife, I would attack that person and fight for as long as I was alive to do so in order to assure her safety and protection.

If someone threatened me with violence, I might respond reciprocally verbally aggressively, but I would absolutely not attack physically unless I was being physically attacked first.

If I witnessed someone being victimized by violence, especially if the person was relatively helpless in the situation, my first choice would be to summon an emergency response to stop the violence. However, if first responders would not be able to arrive quickly enough, and I believed that I could prevent further harm to the victim, I could choose to intervene physically against the perpetrator.

In all of these cases, the violence of my response would be only as violent as was necessary to assure safety. I would aspire to minimize the violence of my response.

I hold it as a strong principle that neither I nor anyone should commit violence in anger. If I am feeling anger, that tells me that I'm not clear-headed enough to rationally judge whether a situation merits a violent response in accordance with my principles. If I am feeling anger, I hold it as a non-negotiable principle that I will not commit violence, even if the situation appears to me to meet a principle that would justify a violent response.

If I ever have to make a choice to take violent action in accordance with my principles, the choice needs to be made with clarity and rationality.

Overall, if I ever commit violence again, it will be because it seems to me to be the *only* way in which to protect someone I love. I believe that there is no acceptable reason to commit violence against a human except to protect a human.

I hope to never again be involved with violence and to never have any reason to resort to violence.

More generally, the principles closest to my heart are to treat every person I encounter with compassion, forgiveness, kindness, and care.

I aspire for every interaction that I have with another human, no matter how trivial the interaction, to be a moment of healing for both of us. I certainly don't manage to live up to this principle all of the time, though I do well with it most of the time. This principle is an aspirational one for me, and I need to also exercise my principle of forgiveness (for myself) when I don't live up to it.

I have a principle to make choices that bring healing and peace to humanity and our planet.

Now let's explore your principles:

- In what instances, if any, would you respond with violence?

- In what instances, if any, would you initiate violence?

- Against whom would you *never* commit violence?

- Against whom would you be willing to take violent action?

- In what instances do you consider it to be unacceptable to take violent action?

- In what instances do you consider it to be acceptable to take violent action?

- What principles do you hold in relation to anger, especially in relation to violence?

- What principles do you hold in regard to weapons?

- What principles do you hold in regard to alcohol or drugs, especially as these relate to violence?

- What other principles do you hold in regard to violence?

- What other principles do you hold in your life
  more generally? (Other principles that you hold
  for your life might inform your principles in
  relation to violence.)

Take the time that you need to become clear about
your principles and to get to know them so well that
they become a part of who you are. Once you reach this
point, you can revisit this practice occasionally if you
want to review or tweak a principle, but in contrast to
the other practices in this book that could be repeated
indefinitely, there is little benefit to repeating this
practice frequently once you know your principles
well.

Contemplative Practice 2: Peaceful Loving Compassion Through the Felt Sense

An audio narration of this practice is available on the "Resources" page of www.peacefulmanbook.com, or it can also be accessed directly by scanning this QR code.

Start by holding yourself in your awareness, and notice what is actually in your awareness when you hold "yourself" in it.

Notice thoughts arising. You don't need to do anything with them or linger on them. Just notice them as they arise.

Notice emotions arising or still lingering in your awareness from earlier. Again, just notice them.

Notice sensations in your body, which could be as simple as the movement of your breath or the pressure of your contact with the floor or against the surface on which you're sitting. The sensations that you notice could also be much subtler.

Bring into your awareness a felt sense of love, compassion, goodwill, benevolence, or peacefulness, whichever of those words has the most resonance and felt sense for you. How does peaceful loving compassion feel to you? How does it feel in your body?

Hold this feeling of love, compassion, goodwill, benevolence, or peacefulness (hereby referred to as peaceful loving compassion) in your awareness for a long moment, and tune in to the texture, the felt sense, and the boundaries of it in your awareness.

Let this feeling of peaceful loving compassion spread throughout your whole body. Let it spread through your torso, including your heart. Down each arm into your fingers. Through your neck and throughout your head. Down each leg into your toes. Feel this peaceful loving compassion spreading and flowing throughout your body.

(At this point, if you are struggling to feel a "felt sense" of peaceful loving compassion in your body, you might choose to skip this practice and go to Contemplative Practice 3. It is a similar meditation, but the process is based on words rather than a "felt sense" in the body. Some people prefer this meditation that works with the felt sense, but others much prefer the language-orientation of Contemplative Practice 3.)

Now imagine that you have a "volume knob" for your peaceful loving compassion, and imagine that you turn up the intensity of the peaceful loving compassion by a couple of notches. How did that visualization work for you? How does the loving compassion feel to you now? Would it feel right to turn it up even a little bit more? (The "volume" visualization works well for some people and not for others; let it go if it doesn't resonate for you.)

Let the peaceful loving compassion encompass your whole self, including both your body and your mind.

Once you have a solid felt sense of peaceful loving compassion, bring to mind a time that you have felt hurt by someone. (If this is your one of your first few times doing this practice, start by working with a time that you were mildly hurt by someone, either emotionally or physically. As you work with this practice and you develop a stronger felt sense of peaceful loving compassion, you can move on to more intense situations until you work up to the most severe violence you have ever experienced, but start with something mild.)

Hold this situation in which you felt hurt in your mind, and feel into what you experienced and experience still in this hurt. What felt sense do you have in your body as you hold this hurt in awareness? What do you feel in relation to the person who hurt you? Let yourself fully feel whatever arises.

Now, bring this hurt that you felt, physical or emotional, into your peaceful, loving compassionate awareness. Cradle the hurt that you feel or felt in your peaceful loving compassion.

How does this hurt feel being held in peaceful loving compassion?

How do you feel as you hold this hurt in peaceful loving compassion?

Take as much time as feels right to you to hold this hurt in peaceful loving compassion.

Bring the person or people who hurt you into your awareness, and hold them in peaceful loving compassion. Notice what arises for you when you do so. If you feel resistance, resentment, anger, fear, or any such adverse emotion arise within yourself, let go of this person from your awareness and instead immediately bring the adverse emotion that you felt arise into your felt sense of peaceful loving compassion.

Cradle the resistance, resentment, anger, or fear in peaceful loving compassion. What unfolds for this emotion as you cradle it in peaceful loving compassion?

If you do remain grounded in peaceful loving compassion as you hold the person or people who hurt you in your field of peaceful loving compassion, how does it feel to you to do so? Once you've explored in detail how it feels within yourself, how do you imagine it feels to this person or these people to be held in your peaceful loving compassion?

Bring into your awareness the entire situation or context in which this hurt happened to you, and hold all of it — your hurt, your whole self, the other people involved, and the whole situation — in peaceful loving compassion.

Keep holding all of this there for as long as feels right to you.

When you feel ready to do so, release the hurt, the people involved, and this whole situation from your awareness.

Come back to just holding yourself in peaceful loving compassion for a moment. Return to noticing the sensations in your body.

Once you're again feeling solid in your peaceful loving compassion as you cradle just yourself in it, bring into your awareness a situation in which you hurt someone else. (As before, if this is one of your first few times doing this practice, start by bringing to awareness a time that you hurt someone relatively mildly, either emotionally or physically. Build up to working on the more severe violence and then the most severe violence that you have ever committed as you repeat this practice. Only move on to severe violence that you have committed when you are solid in your felt sense of peaceful loving compassion even as you process challenging content.)

Hold in mind this situation in which you hurt someone and feel into what you experienced and experience still. What felt sense do you have in your body as you hold this situation in awareness? What do you feel in relation to the person whom you hurt? Let yourself fully feel whatever arises.

Cradle this person whom you hurt in your felt sense of peaceful loving compassion. Infuse their being with peaceful loving compassion.

How do you feel holding this person in peaceful loving compassion? Notice what arises for you. How do you imagine that this person feels being held in your peaceful loving compassion?

Stay with this for as long as it feels right for you to do so.

Now, bring into your awareness how you yourself hurt this other person, and hold yourself in peaceful loving compassion for the violence that you committed. Cradle both the version of yourself that hurt this person in the past and yourself here in this present moment who is remembering.

How does it feel to you to hold yourself in peaceful loving compassion for having hurt someone? Allow yourself to absorb this peaceful loving compassion that you are offering to yourself. If you notice that you are judging yourself for having hurt this person or feeling like you don't deserve peaceful loving compassion, hold those judgements and sentiments in peaceful loving compassion too. Stay with this until it feels complete to you.

Next, bring into your awareness the entire situation or context in which you hurt this person, and hold all of this — the other person, the other person's hurt, yourself, the whole situation — in peaceful loving compassion.

Let this whole situation become saturated with peaceful loving compassion. When that happens or you just feel complete with this process for right now, let this situation go from your awareness.

To complete this practice of peaceful loving compassion for right now, come back to holding your present-moment self in peaceful loving compassion for a moment. Turn up the volume of the peaceful loving compassion again, if that visualization works for you. Let the intensity of the peaceful loving compassion clear out any remainders in your system from the situations that you brought to mind.

Contemplative Practice 3: Peaceful Loving Compassion Through Language

An audio narration of this practice is available on the "Resources" page of www.peacefulmanbook.com. It can also be accessed directly by scanning this QR code.

If the above practice worked well for you and you had a clear felt sense of peaceful loving compassion, there is no need for you to do this practice as well. It is similar to the previous practice but uses words rather than a felt sense. This version of the practice is for those who find it smoother to work with language than with feeling sensations.

Start by holding yourself in your awareness. Notice what is actually in your awareness when you hold "yourself" in it.

Notice thoughts arising. You don't need to do anything with them or linger on them. Just notice thoughts as they arise.

Notice emotions that are arising or that are still lingering in your awareness from earlier. Again, you're just noticing.

Notice sensations in your body, which could be as simple as the movement of your breath or the pressure of your contact with the floor or against the surface on which you're sitting.

Begin to repeat to yourself, "May I be peaceful. May I love and be loved. May I heal."

Repeat these words and direct them to yourself, over and over and over. Notice what you feel as you continue to repeat these words. Stay with this repetition for a long moment.

Next, bring to mind a person towards whom you feel warmly, and begin to direct a similar phrase towards this person you brought to mind: "May you be peaceful. May you love and be loved. May you heal."

Repeat these words many times, directed towards this person towards whom you feel warmly. Stay with this repetition for a long moment too.

Now bring to mind a time that you have felt hurt by someone. (If this is your one of your first few times doing this practice, start by working with a time that you were mildly hurt by someone, either emotionally or physically. After several repetitions of this practice, start moving on to more intense situations and work up to the most severe violence you have ever experienced slowly over many repetitions of this practice.)

Holding this hurt version of yourself in your awareness, repeat the phrase again, directed towards the hurt part of yourself: "May you be peaceful. May you love and be loved. May you heal." Stay with this repetition to the hurt part of yourself for a while.

How does it feel to the hurt part of yourself to have this phrase repeated to it?

Bring the person or people who hurt you into your awareness, and repeat this phrase to them: "May you be peaceful. May you love and be loved. May you heal." It's of course optimal if you truly wish these words for the person or people who hurt you, but the practice can still be healing and effective even if you feel stretched to wish peace and love towards these people. Just keep repeating the phrase to them in your mind.

How do you feel extending these wishes to the people who hurt you?

How do you imagine they feel hearing this wish from you?

Stay with this repetition to the person or people who hurt you for as long as feels right to you.

When you feel ready to do so, release this hurt and the people involved with it from your awareness.

Focus your awareness just on yourself and repeat this phrase to yourself again several times: "May I be peaceful. May I love and be loved. May I heal."

When you feel refreshed with these wishes for yourself and ready to continue, bring to mind a situation in which you hurt someone else. (Again, if this is one of your first few times doing this practice, start by bringing to awareness a time that you hurt someone relatively mildly, either emotionally or physically. Build up to working on the more severe violence and then the most severe violence that you have ever committed as you repeat this practice over time.)

Hold the person who you hurt in your awareness, and repeat to this person, "May you be peaceful. May you love and be loved. May you heal."

How do you feel extending these wishes to the person who you hurt?

How do you imagine this person feels hearing this

phrase from you?

Stay with this repetition to the person that you hurt until it feels complete to you.

Begin to repeat this phrase to the version of yourself from the past who hurt this person: "May you be peaceful. May you love and be loved. May you heal."

How does it feel to the past version of yourself who hurt this person to hear this phrase repeated to it?

How do you feel repeating these words to this version of yourself who hurt someone in the past?

Once you feel complete with this repetition, come back to right here and now, and again repeat to the current version of yourself, "May I be peaceful. May I love and be loved. May I heal."

May you be peaceful. May you love and be loved. May you heal.

Contemplative Practice 4: Healing All Victims of Violence Globally, Within Yourself

An audio narration of this practice is available on the "Resources" page of www.peacefulmanbook.com. It can also be accessed directly by scanning this QR code.

This practice can be intense. You need to have some resilience and steadiness to do it and remain fully present in your body and in a state of peacefulness. Please only do this practice when you feel ready for it. Practices 2 and 3 are good ones to do to build up to this practice.

When you are able to remain present in your body and peaceful throughout this practice, it can be healing, for you, for your loved ones, for all men, and for the whole world.

Start by noticing the space inside your chest where your heart is located. Simply notice how this space feels to you. What sensations arise in your chest with your awareness focused on this space? What emotional quality do you feel?

Infuse this space that holds your heart with love and compassion. Keep sending love and compassion into your heart space, and then let your heart bathe in the love and compassion until it is saturated. Then, let your heart radiate the love and compassion out to your whole body, your whole self, and the whole world. Stay with this feeling for a long moment.

Let the love and compassion pouring out of your heart infuse right back into your heart. Let your heart become an overflowing vessel of love and compassion.

When you have a strong felt sense of love and compassion in your heart, bring into your awareness a time when you have been a victim of violence. Hold this violence and what you experienced in your awareness. Notice how your body feels with this violence in your awareness.

Now, put the violence that you experienced inside of your heart, which is filled with love and compassion. Put your whole self from the past who was the victim of this violence into your heart.

Let the violence that you experienced and your whole self be surrounded by love and compassion, all held inside your heart.

If it feels right, let the love and compassion infuse, merge with, and consume the violence that you experienced, in the way that flames surround and consume wood in a fire. As the violence is consumed by love and compassion, let it and the suffering that came with it be transmuted into peacefulness, love, and compassion. Let this process of transmutation run until it feels complete.

Then, release the peacefulness, love, and compassion that you have generated in your heart through your whole body, your whole being.

How does this feel?

Let that go, and take another moment to feel and reconnect with your heart, filled with love and compassion.

Now, bring into your awareness how people about whom you care have been victims of violence. Since this book is focused on male-to-male violence, consider how your father, your brothers, your sons, your uncles, your cousins, your nephews, and your friends have experienced violence. (It can of course be a powerful practice to do this for female loved ones as well, but that isn't the focus of this book.)

Bring into your heart all of the violence these loved ones have experienced. If you don't know any details of their experiences of violence, use your imagination and your felt sense of the violence and suffering that they might have experienced.

Let all of this violence committed against the men and boys that you love and care about be surrounded by the love and compassion overflowing in your heart.

All of the violence experienced by your loved ones gets consumed by the love and compassion in your heart like wood in a fire. Let the violence be transmuted into peacefulness, love, and compassion in your heart.

Allow this transmutation of violence into peace to take whatever time it needs, as the love and compassion in your heart re-form everything that they touch into peacefulness.

When the transmutation is complete, radiate the newly generated peacefulness, compassion, and love out of your heart back to your loved ones who experienced the violence originally. Send this transmuted love and compassion to them in their lives as healings and blessings.

Stay with this radiating until it feels complete.

Take another moment to feel and reconnect with your heart that is filled with love and compassion until you're ready to move on. If you feel that you have gone far enough with this practice for right now, feel free to stop here and save the later part of this practice for another time.

If you're ready to continue, bring into your awareness all of the violence that all men and all boys have experienced throughout the entire history of *Homo sapiens* and all of the violence that men and boys are experiencing even right now, over the entirety of planet Earth.

Hold all of this violence that has been experienced by male *Homo sapiens* in your awareness. Hold all of their suffering that results from violence in your awareness.

If you feel prepared to do so, bring all of this violence that you're holding in your awareness into your heart that is filled with love and compassion. (If you don't feel ready to bring all of this violence into your heart, send it back out of your awareness, around the world, and to where it belongs in time. Feel all of the violence and all of the suffering blowing back out of your awareness the way a strong wind blows the leaves off a tree in autumn and scatters them. Stay with this blowing and scattering until you feel clear of the violence and suffering from your awareness.)

Let all of the violence that the males of the *Homo sapiens* species have ever experienced, which is now held in your heart, be surrounded by the love and compassion there. Let the violence be infused and consumed by the love and compassion. Love consumes the violence the way that fire consumes wood, producing more love and compassion out of the violence.

There's been so much violence throughout our history, but there's also so much love and compassion in our hearts.

Let all of this violence and suffering transmute into peacefulness, love, and compassion. Let it take the time that it needs. Your heart is likely becoming more and more full of love and compassion as the violence metamorphosizes into peaceful loving compassion.

When you feel this process of transmutation in your heart to be complete for now, let your heart radiate out all of this love and compassion that has been generated out of violence to all the boys and men all around the planet and across all of time.

Let every male human alive today and who has ever lived receive the love and compassion that is radiating from your heart, inviting them towards their own healing from violence as their hearts are ready.

Feel how it is for all of this compassion and love to radiate from your heart to all these boys and men, inviting peace, love, and compassion among our human brotherhood.

Contemplative Practice 5: Healing All Violence Committed Globally, Within Yourself

An audio narration of this practice is available on the "Resources" page of www.peacefulmanbook.com, or it can be accessed directly by scanning this QR code.

Like the previous practice, this one can be intense. In fact, this one can be more intense for some than the previous one. It is focused on the healing of violent actors. Please proceed with it only when you feel ready for it.

To start this practice, notice the space inside your chest where your heart sits. What sensations do you feel in your chest with your awareness focused on this space? What emotional quality do you experience?

Infuse this space that holds your heart with waves of love and compassion. Keep sending love and compassion into your heart space, and let your heart keep receiving this love and compassion. When it's overflowing with love and compassion, let your heart radiate all of this love and compassion to your whole body, to your mind, to your whole self, to your loved ones, to all of humanity, to all of life, and to the whole planet.

Once you feel a clear sense of love and compassion in your heart, bring into your awareness a time that you committed violent against someone. Hold in your awareness this violence that you committed and how you felt when you did so. Notice how your body feels right now with this violence that you committed in your awareness.

Notice how the violence that you committed resulted from your own suffering in some way, most likely from fear or anger.

Once you have this violence you committed and the suffering clearly in mind, bring them into your heart, which is overflowing with love and compassion. Right now, it is to you for the violence that you yourself committed that we are bringing compassion. This practice is not about the person whom you hurt. In this practice, we're inviting love and compassion for you, even in the moments when you have been violent. This does not excuse or condone the violence you committed, but it's love and compassion for you for violence that you committed, even if the violence was not acceptable according to your principles.

Let the violence that you committed and your own suffering related to this violence be surrounded by love and compassion, all held inside your heart.

Allow the love and compassion to infuse, merge with, and consume the violence that you committed, in the way that flames surround and consume wood in a fire. As your violence is consumed by love and compassion, let it be transmuted into peacefulness, love, and compassion.

Let this take the time that it needs for the transmutation to unfold. When it feels complete to you (at least for right now), release the transmuted peacefulness, love, and compassion from your heart through your whole body and being.

Register how this feels in your body, and then take another moment to feel and reconnect with your heart, still full of love and compassion.

When you feel ready to continue, bring into your awareness violence that has been committed by males you know and about whom you care. Have your brothers, sons, father, uncles, cousins, nephews, grandfathers, or grandsons committed violence? Have friends of yours committed violence? (For the purpose of this practice, knowing accurate details is not important.)

Notice how the violence that these males committed came from a place of suffering within themselves, usually coming from fear or anger.

Bring into your heart all of the violence that these males close to you have committed. Also bring into your heart the suffering that led them to commit violence. Let this violence and suffering be surrounded by love and compassion, overflowing in your heart.

Let all of this violence committed by males you care about be consumed by the love and compassion in your heart like wood in a fire, and let it be transmuted into peacefulness, love, and compassion.

Allow this transmutation from violence to peace to take whatever time it needs. Let the love and compassion in your heart transmute everything that they touch into peacefulness.

When the transmutation feels complete, let your heart radiate the newly generated peacefulness, compassion, and love out of your heart back to all those you care about who committed the violence originally. Send this generated love and compassion to them in their lives as healings and blessings.

Then, let that go, and take another moment to just feel and reconnect with your heart, filled with love and compassion. Take a moment to reset and ground yourself, to simply be aware of the love and compassion in your heart.

Next, bring into your awareness all of the violence that all men and all boys have committed throughout the history of humanity and even the violence that is being committed right at this moment the world over. Hold all of this violence in your awareness.

If (and only if) you feel prepared to do so, bring all of the violence that has ever been committed by human men and boys from your awareness into your heart. (If you don't feel ready to bring all of this violence into your heart, send it back out of your awareness, around the world and to where it belongs in time. Feel it all blowing back out of your awareness the way a strong wind blows the leaves off of a tree in autumn and scatters them. Stay with the blowing and scattering until your awareness feels clear.)

Let all of this violence now held in your heart be surrounded by the love and compassion there. Let the violence be infused and consumed by the love and compassion. As the violence is consumed by love and compassion, notice how it is transmuted into yet more love and compassion. Give this process the time that it needs to unfold.

There's so much violence, but so much love and

compassion reside in the heart.

When you feel that this process of transmutation in your heart is complete for now, let your heart radiate all of this love and compassion that has just been generated out to all of the boys and all of the men who have ever committed violence, all around the planet and across all of time.

Feel how it is for you for all of this compassion and love to radiate from your heart to all these boys and men. You are inviting peace, love, and compassion to our human brotherhood. Keep radiating the love and compassion from your heart until the sending feels complete.

Contemplative Practice 6: Forgiveness

Forgiveness is the release of tension and hardened adverse emotions such as resentment, guilt, horror, shame, and anger that have been held in the heart, the body, and the mind. Forgiveness is dissolving the desire for revenge or for harm to come to a person. Forgiveness lets go of the past to enable a more peaceful and beautiful present and future.

The primary purpose of forgiveness is to heal the forgiver. Forgiveness clears the forgiver of old tensions and armoring around the heart. Forgiveness may sometimes benefit the forgiven if you still have a relationship with that person, but often forgiveness has no effect on the forgiven. You forgive someone for your own liberation and your own healing.

Forgiveness frees you, refreshes you, and opens you to new possibilities for peacefulness, passion, love, purpose, and bliss.

Forgiveness is not denying anger and other emotions or sending them away. We need to fully acknowledge and feel all of our emotions before we can forgive the person who committed the transgression that caused the emotions. Inviting forgiveness accepts the emotions and gives them space to move and find their own organic completion, rather than keeping them locked in our hearts, bodies, and minds.

To forgive does not mean to condone an action that you deem unacceptable according to your principles. In this practice of forgiveness, we forgive the person who was violent, not the act of violence. The act of violence can still be held as an unacceptable transgression even as we forgive the person who performed the action.

You can forgive yourself too for your past actions of violence, even if your actions were out of alignment with your principles.

There is no obligation for you to forgive anyone, including yourself. True forgiveness cannot be forced. It can only be invited. Putting a "should" on forgiveness only hardens the stuck emotions.

Sometimes exploring forgiveness will bring up even stronger feelings of anger, resentment, or other challenging emotions. This too is part of the healing process because it enables you to gain greater awareness of these emotions and to feel them more fully. If this happens, acknowledge the arising emotions and welcome them if you can. They're the truth of your experience right now. There is no urgency whatsoever for you to reach a state of forgiveness. Whatever arises is part of the forgiveness practice and the healing process.

An audio narration of the following practice is available on the "Resources" page of www.peacefulmanbook.com, or it can be accessed directly by scanning this QR code.

To start this forgiveness practice, bring to mind an instance in which you committed an act for which you still feel guilt, shame, self-judgement, or remorse. Notice the sensations in your body that you feel when you think about your act. Also be aware of the pain that you may have caused another person as a result of your action. What emotions and sensations arise in you as you consider this?

After feeling this for a moment, invite all of the emotions and sensations you feel about your action to release as you say to yourself, "I forgive you." If it feels right, you could follow that with a vow that you won't do any such harm to others again. How does this feel?

In this practice, you're not asking someone else to forgive you. You are exploring forgiveness of yourself.

Repeat "I forgive you" and send positive regard to yourself until this feels complete to you for right now.

What sensations arise in your body? What emotions are you feeling? How does your heart feel?

When you're ready to proceed to the second part of this forgiveness practice, bring to mind someone towards whom you feel resentment, anger, or another challenging emotion. Start with someone who violated you in a relatively minor way and towards whom you feel only a small amount of resentment or anger. Notice the emotions and sensations that you have in relation to this person for whatever they did to you.

Next, invite all of these feelings related to this person to release, and in your mind, tell this person, "I forgive you."

See how it feels in your body to say, "I forgive you," to this person in your imagination, and observe what unfolds for you next. Remember that you're forgiving the person, not their actions.

You may feel in your body the warmth and softening of forgiveness flowing through you, or you may not. Either case can be welcomed as part of the practice.

If anger arises as you're doing this practice (and it commonly does), acknowledge the anger, accept it, and welcome it. Don't feed it or enflame it, but allow it space to unfold. This too is part of your healing process. You're learning more about your true emotions and your holdings. Invite compassion for yourself for what you're feeling right now.

What's most important and powerfully healing in this forgiveness practice is the *invitation* you give to yourself to soften into forgiveness. The *feeling* of softening into forgiveness that sometimes follows is of course healing and valuable too, but it's secondary to the intention and invitation.

If telling "I forgive you" to this person in your imagination for the first time was too upsetting or triggering to you, end this practice here for the time being. Otherwise, keep repeating "I forgive you" in your imagination to the person as many times as feels right to you in this moment, sending them positive regard and wishes for their well-being every time you repeat it.

What sensations do you feel in your body? What emotions do you feel? How does your heart feel?

You can repeat this part of the practice for others towards whom you feel more resentment or anger as you feel drawn and slowly build towards forgiveness of those who have been violent with you in the most severe ways.

May this practice lead you to the peacefulness and love that can arise out of forgiveness.

Conclusion

The stories I shared in the first part of this book are about the violence I experienced and committed. I haven't explicitly told the stories of my healing journey in this book, but the practices for healing in Parts 2 and 3 are implicitly the stories of my own healing work. These are practices that I have used at different times over the past twenty years to transform layers of trauma into healing.

I believe that healing from violence or any other trauma is a life-long process. There is no final "healed" state. There are perpetually deeper levels of healing that may only become apparent later. As we evolve our consciousnesses, deeper healing becomes available to us.

May the words of this book be a salve for any trauma that you have experienced and that still lives in you. May my experiences with violence and the words of this book be an invitation for you and for all of us as men to find peace, healing, and compassion within ourselves.

May you heal and be free of the violence of your past and from any violence in the future. May we create peace together.

Final Notes

If you benefited from this book and you believe that other men who have experienced violence could benefit from it as well, please help these others to discover it by leaving a sincere review on the platform on which you obtained this book. Sincere reviews will help this book not only to reach more men but to reach the men who most need support with healing from violence.

Ultimately, I hope that this book supports so many men on their healing journeys that our world becomes a more peaceful place for all. Your review can make a small contribution to this.

If you are interested in receiving occasional updates on courses, individual sessions, and other news related to healing from violence and The Peaceful Man book, please go to www.peacefulmanbook.com and subscribe to the newsletter.

About the Author

Since 2014, Brad has been teaching and supporting other men on their healing journeys by facilitating groups and through individual coaching sessions that include body-based healing experiences and contemplative practices. Brad has received extensive training and holds certifications in developmental coaching, somatic practices, group facilitation, and transformative change.

Brad believes that helping men to heal from violence and to find peace within themselves is a key to enabling humanity and all of life on earth to flourish. He wrote this book in service of this vision and as a means of helping men like you to embark on journeys of healing.

In addition to authoring The Peaceful Man, Brad offers individual online sessions and group courses to help those looking to heal from violence. You can find out more about Brad's work and his book at www.peacefulmanbook.com.

72785907R00118